Don't Call it L[i

CW00918527

'Every teacher in English is a teacher of Er
one of the early school inspectors, back in 1921. It's never been truer, or more relevant.

Literacy has a major impact on young people's life-chances and it is every teacher's responsibility to help build their communication, reading and writing skills. However, this book isn't just about literacy; it's also about what great teachers do in their classrooms, about applying knowledge consistently across classrooms, in order to help pupils to become more confident in all their subjects.

This book shows every teacher – whatever your subject – the simple steps which could transform your students into better speakers, listeners, readers and writers. Harnessing a range of straightforward but powerful techniques, it shows you how to help each student in your subject to improve their spelling, to use the key vocabulary of your subject more accurately and to speak, read and write with confidence like a historian, scientist, designer or mathematician.

The book is structured into clear sections, which are then divided into short, easy-to-absorb units on the classroom implications of what we know about literacy. *Don't Call it Literacy!* also includes:

- language commentaries which exemplify points made by the author;
- talking points at the end of each unit for self-assessment;
- a glossary for non-specialists;
- subject specific vocabulary for building students' word power;
- tutor time spellings lists;
- a reading list on teaching, language, literacy and education.

Written by a leading authority in the field, this book will help both trainee and practising secondary school teachers to turn their classrooms into literacy-friendly environments, increasing the motivation and achievement of their students.

Geoff Barton is Headteacher of King Edward VI School, a large comprehensive school in Suffolk, UK. He has written and edited more than fifty books on grammar and literature, is also a Founding Fellow of the English Association, and a regular writer and speaker on English, literacy and school leadership.

Don't Call it Literacy!

What every teacher needs to
know about speaking, listening,
reading and writing

Geoff Barton

Routledge
Taylor & Francis Group

LONDON AND NEW YORK

First published 2013
by Routledge
2 Park Square, Milton Park, Abingdon, Oxon OX14 4RN

Simultaneously published in the USA and Canada
by Routledge
711 Third Avenue, New York, NY 10017

*Routledge is an imprint of the Taylor & Francis Group,
an informa business*

British Library Cataloguing in Publication Data
A catalogue record for this book is available from the
British Library

Library of Congress Cataloging in Publication Data
Barton, Geoff.
    Don't call it literacy!: what every teacher needs to know
    about speaking, listening, reading and writing/Geoff Barton.
    p. cm.
    1. Literacy – Great Britain. 2. Language arts – Great Britain.
    I. Title.
    LC156.G7.B37 2012
    302.2'2440941 – dc23
    2012026091

ISBN: 978-0-415-53602-8 (hbk)
ISBN: 978-0-415-53603-5 (pbk)
ISBN: 978-0-203-11200-7 (ebk)

Typeset in Celeste and Optima
by Florence Production Ltd, Stoodleigh, Devon

Printed and bound by CPI Group (UK) Ltd, Croydon, CR0 4YY

'The limits of my language are the limits of my world'
Ludwig Wittgenstein (1889–1951)

Contents

Contents

Contents

Appendices

Introduction

Why literacy matters

This is a book about literacy that is not really about literacy. That's a decoy. It's actually about what great teachers do in their classrooms, about what we might quaintly call teaching and learning.

We need to get that admission out in the open from the start because one problem with previous approaches to whole-school literacy was that we called it literacy. Words matter, and the word 'literacy' too often creates all the wrong impressions.

Here's an example: if you were to suggest in your school that you should devote the next staff training day to the theme of literacy, what would the reaction be? Polite indifference? A cynical rolling of the eyes? A frustrated snort of collective derision? Or, perhaps, outright hostility? My guess is you wouldn't receive a spontaneous round of applause.

That's because many teachers would say, or at least think, 'But we did literacy a few years ago'. And perhaps they would visualise the stack of fading yellow ring-binders being used to prop up a sagging shelf in the English stock cupboard: the literacy graveyard.

But, in truth, we haven't really 'done' literacy, or, in most schools, even started to 'do' it. If we had, there wouldn't be a scandalous number of young people leaving our schools each year unable to write a simple set of instructions or a report or a letter which didn't contain errors of punctuation and spelling, without a tone that was too personal or colloquial, and without the sense of assured clarity and confidence that comes from knowing what good writing is.

In fact, if we're going to be really honest with each other, too many of our teachers would struggle to do it too.

Similarly, if we had 'done' literacy, we wouldn't have youngsters who misread basic written accounts of events, who haven't the resilience to read to the end of a text of, say, 800 words, and who lack the strategies that you and I would take for granted in reading a leaflet for specific advice (scanning), or an article for the gist (skimming), or who would think the idea of sitting down with a book in their hands as an alien and perverse activity.

No: we most certainly haven't 'done' literacy.

And that's what this book is about – the literacy skills we need as teachers, the small bits of knowledge which, if we apply them consistently across our classrooms, will help our pupils to become more confident in our subject as well as in their more general skills of speaking, listening, thinking, reading and writing, as well as the skills we need for our own day-to-day work in, say, explaining, questioning and writing reports.

Who the book is for

I've written the book for those we might call 'real teachers' – that is, people who are in the classroom working with young people pretty much every day. You are the people I work with at school and who I meet on the courses I occasionally run and at the conferences I'm occasionally wheeled out to speak at.

You are the kind of people who, many years ago, taught me and made me want to become a teacher.

Most of what I have learned in 28 or so years as a teacher myself tells me that whatever the ebb and flow of educational wacky wheezes, of fads and fashions, and from watching the revolving doors of Secretaries of State for Education, it's the stuff we do in the classroom that changes children's lives. This, more than big policy initiatives and strategies and announcements, is what makes a difference.

It's all about the classroom. After all, many of us became teachers because we were ourselves taught by great teachers. That, I suspect, continues to be the case: teachers continue to inspire young people. They choose to become teachers themselves not because of a new policy or strategy or initiative, or even because of the curriculum: it's because of what their own teachers did, how they behaved and spoke, of how they inspired us.

I'm going to suggest that at the heart of the success of these influential teachers is the way they use language. It's how they explain, how they give instructions and pose questions, how they pause and use silence, and how, perhaps unknowingly, they unlock the language skills of their pupils to help them to become successful learners.

Speaking at the annual conference of the ASCL (the Association of School and College Leaders) a few years ago, the Chief Executive of the RSA (the Royal Society for the Encouragement of Arts, Manufactures and Commerce), Matthew Taylor, made a light-hearted but I suspect profound aside. He said he thought that young people today were likely to be less tolerant of poor and mediocre teaching than our generation ever was, but that they still loved being taught by a great teacher.

In other words, back when people like me were at school, we accepted that school would largely be tedious and impersonal. School life was like that. So having a great teacher made an enormous and sometimes literally life-changing impact.

Education good guy Ian Gilbert synthesised this in the title of his book: *Why Do I Need a Teacher When I've Got Google?*

Students now don't need teachers as we did in the past: information is available to them without us, so long as they have reliable techniques for sifting the reliable from the dubious.

And yet, and yet: experience suggests that the human dimension of a great teacher – someone who knows a lot of stuff and can explain it to us – still counts for a lot.

Introduction

If we synthesise what made our own 'teachers of influence' great, I suspect we'll come back to a small number of key ingredients, with language often at their hidden core.

First, these teachers will have struck us as experts. In the eighteenth century, poet Oliver Goldsmith described the attitude of the pupils to the Village Schoolmaster:

And still they gaz'd and still the wonder grew,
That one small head could carry all he knew.

Yet I suspect we have all been taught by teachers who were both experts in their subject and were terrible teachers. Subject expertise in itself isn't enough.

Our most effective teachers will, as well as knowing their subject, have used the specialised vocabulary of their subject: it's one way that we will have identified them as experts. Yet this in itself isn't enough. Great teachers don't just use big words. It's about teaching – not just using – the specialist vocabulary of our subject.

That means knowing the key vocabulary, the nouns, verbs and connectives, that help us to express our knowledge in the language of the expert or enthusiast.

They won't have called it literacy, of course; it was simply how they taught. It was the way they explained and clarified and simplified; how they asked and answered our questions; how they knew when to talk and when to let us do the talking; how they knew what kind of feedback to give us and what the appropriate language for this might be.

And in the process they will have made us feel that we were special and that their subject – whatever it was – was something compelling and fascinating, that we wanted to be involved in learning more about it.

All of this is what great teachers did and what they do. And although on the surface it seems to be about subject knowledge and expertise, the best teachers are gifted communicators and motivators: they use language with an apparently effortless ability to help their pupils to respond and learn.

And that's what this book is about and why I'm suggesting we 'don't call it literacy': instead, let's share the implicit approaches and techniques that great teachers use and see if we can't make them explicit by demystifying some of their language traits.

How this book works

Because I'm writing this book for teachers, I'm conscious that you won't have much time to spare. And if you did, I think I would probably prefer you to devote it to reading, say, a good novel or a book that deepened your sense of expertise in your own subject.

I'm not therefore trying to provide you with a history of whole-school literacy here, or a weighty reference to academic papers on the subject. Instead, rather simply, I'm hoping to provide a practical handbook of ideas that work in the classroom – by which I mean helping teachers to teach better and pupils to learn more effectively.

Someone once quipped of the poet Philip Larkin, 'He was miserable so that you don't have to be.' Well, I've used a similar approach with this book. Over the past few years I've read hundreds of books, articles and papers about literacy and my feeling is that I've read them so that you don't have to. I've tried to absorb the theories I've read, combine them with the teaching I've seen and done, and produce something that leads to action in the classroom.

That's not to say I'm anti-academic. I enjoy reading books and articles about literacy. I like the idea of building my own expertise. But essentially I see the majority of my readers as experts in their subjects – teachers who want to devote their own research to understanding more about Maths or History or Science, and not to feeling that they also have to absorb complicated theory about language and linguistics.

So I'm aiming to write with a light touch, but with a strong sense of voice. I'm not going to shy away from giving my views or pretend to be impartial on certain matters (I happen, for example, to think that the concept of 'multiple intelligence' when applied to classrooms is pretty fatuous).

But if you feel there are areas of the topics that you want to get more insight into, then I have included a brief reading list at the end. These are texts I actively recommend, rather than those that I have merely read, so that you can devote meaningful time to them if interested, knowing that they contain relevant ideas to classroom practice.

One last point about accessibility. I could hardly write a book about literacy and not model the practices that I am recommending. I have therefore written with a careful eye on my reader. I am assuming you will appreciate more white space than black ink on a page, shortish sections, typographical features that aid rapid reading (lists, headings, short paragraphs, bullet points, boxes), and an authorial tone that is neither bland nor over-prescriptive.

That's what I'm trying to do, though – as ever with writing – the process itself always proves a vaguely mystical one in which the words curiously end up writing themselves, writing us. If you write a lot, you'll know precisely what I mean.

The book is structured into clear sections. The sub-sections are then framed by some 'key knowledge'. Then there are short units on the classroom implications of what we know about literacy.

Literacy books don't have a great track-record of being read by anyone but the literacy coordinator and a few hardcore staffroom zealots. I hope this one is different and that you enjoy it. I also hope it's not just being read because Ofsted now has literacy in its sights. Literacy – like most things in schools – is far too important to be reduced to an item on a cheerless Ofsted tick-list.

Most of all – if you'll forgive the lofty idealism – I hope *Don't Call it Literacy!* helps you to teach better and your pupils to learn better.

Geoff Barton
Suffolk

LANGUAGE COMMENTARY

At school many of us were told never to start sentences with 'and' and 'but'. Throughout my introduction I've done just that. I often do. But (see what I mean?) I think I do it for emphasis. The 'but' there is no ordinary 'but': it's serving more like another connective, such as 'however' or the phrase 'despite this'. And I do it (there we go again) because I'm pretty secure in my command of sentence structure. I know that in starting a sentence with one of those conjunctions, I'm doing it for effect; I can rationalise and justify it. With our pupils, except for special effects, it's a general rule that's usually worth reinforcing.

PART ONE

Literacy essentials

This part is designed to establish the territory: what we mean by literacy, what we should rightfully expect of every teacher, how a school might ensure consistency across every teacher in every subject in every classroom. It has been written to underpin all that follows and, in particular, to lend support to senior leaders and literacy coordinators in their role of establishing consistency of practice across and between classrooms and teachers.

LANGUAGE COMMENTARY

That word 'practice' catches a lot of people out – teachers as much as pupils. Should we use 'practice' or 'practise'?

Some users (those with a secure grammatical grasp) need to be told no more than that the former usage is a noun (as in 'my practice, your practice, the practice') and the latter a verb (as in 'I practise, you practise, she practises'). For many of us, that still doesn't help a lot.

The easiest way to get it right every time is to replace 'practice/practise' in your mind with 'advice/advise', two words that we would be unlikely to use incorrectly: thus 'I need to practise' becomes self-evidently the verb form because we would say 'I need to advise' rather than 'I need to advice'.

What we know about literacy in the UK

Tales of our nation's endemic illiteracy are frequently overstated, especially in certain newspapers. In truth, we have very little genuine illiteracy, if by that we mean people actually unable to read or write at all.

Yet for a highly developed economic country, our national literacy levels can seem alarming. It is a source of considerable surprise, for example, when we read statistics about the state of the nation's reading and writing habits: we see how many children come from backgrounds where expectations of talking, interacting, reading and writing are so very different from what we might consider normal.

We need also, as teachers, to keep feeling angry that after eleven or more years of compulsory education in our schools, something like half of our young people come out unable to achieve a clutch of C grades at GCSE that include the basics of English and Maths. Perhaps, unlike some of our international competitors, we have too easily accepted this as an inevitable norm.

The best picture of our national literacy levels comes from the National Literacy Trust (www.literacytrust.org.uk). In 2010 they produced a comprehensive survey of UK literacy, which they called, grandly, *Literacy: State of the Nation, A picture of literacy in the UK today.*

Literacy essentials

Here are some of its more striking statistics of relevance to us in schools. They are followed by some questions for discussion. These might provide a useful starting-point for reflection in your school or department about the literacy levels of the pupils you work with and their attitudes and backgrounds.

Literacy levels in the UK:

- One in six people in the UK struggle with literacy. This means their literacy is below the level expected of an eleven year old.

Attitudes towards reading and writing:

- 22.2% of young people aged eight to sixteen say they enjoy reading very much and 28.4% say they enjoy it quite a lot. 39.2% say they like it a bit and 10.2% say they do not enjoy reading at all.

- 66% of adults believe that the ability to read, write and communicate is a fundamental right in modern society.

- 92% of the British public say literacy is vital to the economy, and essential for getting a good job.

- A quarter of children and young people do not recognise a link between reading and success.

- Children and young people who engage in technology based texts, such as blogs, enjoy writing more and have more positive attitudes towards writing – 57% express a general enjoyment of writing vs. 40% who don't have a blog.

- There is a consistent gender difference in attitudes towards writing. Boys do not enjoy writing as much as girls (38% vs. 52%), either for family/friends or for schoolwork and are more likely to rate themselves as 'not very good writers' (48% vs. 42%).

- Technology based materials are the most frequently read, with nearly two-thirds of children and young people reading websites every week, and half of children and young people reading emails and blogs/networking websites (such as Bebo, MySpace) every week.

Reading and writing frequency:

- 73% of parents and carers say their child often reads.

- Age is closely linked to attitudes towards reading and reading behaviour. 30% of five to eight year olds read a book every day compared with only 17% of fifteen to seventeen year olds. However, teenagers are more likely to read other materials such as blogs, websites and newspapers.

- 14% of children and young people in lower income homes rarely or never read their books for pleasure.

Parents reading with their children:

- Parents are the most important reading role models for their children and young people. 71% of young people say that their mothers are their most important role model for reading and 62% say their fathers.

- One in five parents easily find the opportunity to read to their children, with the rest struggling to read to their children due to fatigue and busy lifestyles. Of the parents that read to the children, 67% are mothers compared to just 17% of fathers.

- Recent research has shown that the likelihood of fathers reading to their children is linked to their socio-economic background. Fathers with higher incomes are more likely to read to their children, for example, 21% of dads in £40–50k income homes are the principal reader, compared to just 11% in homes with an annual income of £10–15k.

TALKING POINTS

- So how does the national picture for the UK compare with what you know of the pupils who come to your school?
- For pupils coming from backgrounds where conversation, reading and writing are sporadic and perhaps impoverished, what first impressions does your school give of an attitude to talking, reading and writing?
- What do you know of the attitudes of your pupils and parents to, say, reading and writing? How could you find out more?
- How might a survey of pupils' attitudes help to develop further your school or department's approach to the promotion of reading and writing?

How much does a teacher of any subject need to know about literacy?

George Sampson was an educational guru in the days before 'guru' had been poached from its Hindu origins (meaning a spiritual guide) to be used blandly in sentences such as 'George Sampson was an educational guru'.

Sampson was also one of the first school inspectors. Despite that, we forgive him, because in 1921 he wrote something which has become a literacy mantra (another word loan from Hindi, by the way): 'Every teacher in English is a teacher of English' (*English for the English*, Cambridge University Press, 1921). You won't find a literacy consultant who doesn't quack that, probably rather too frequently.

But it is sometimes presented as if we need all of our teachers to be experts in teaching spelling and grammar. We don't. But we do need teachers who are themselves confident communicators, readers and writers and who can then – critically – take the skills they implicitly use and make them explicit to their pupils.

That's essentially the approach in this book – the assumption that, whatever our subject specialism, as teachers we are members of what we might call the 'Literacy Club'. Even the most linguistically insecure of us will be competent readers and writers. Our job is to help our pupils to acquire such competence and turn it into confidence.

Thus, as a teacher of, say, History, I have a responsibility to help my pupils not just to know about history, but to speak, read and write like a historian.

That will involve having some specialist knowledge – for example, the conventions of historical writing and of the ways that historians themselves write about history. But more important will be an analytical self-awareness, which allows us to identify how we speak, read and write about history so that those skills can then be made explicit for our youngsters.

In this approach teachers' literacy responsibilities are akin to an apprenticeship model: we are passing on the skills from an older generation to a younger one, and, as I argue throughout this book, that is best done through a process of demystifying what we do – explaining, demonstrating, modelling, teaching and giving feedback. It's the stuff of teaching – the things great teachers do in their subjects all the time. Now it's time to make our literacy expertise more explicit for our pupils.

Later parts of the book explore some of the specific knowledge associated with teaching ways of reading and types of writing. For now I am concerned with what we might term generic skills – the kind of skills and knowledge we should expect of every teacher in every subject. These, I would suggest, ought to form part of a school's core expectations of its teachers and teaching assistants and be embedded in induction, training and performance management.

Twelve generic areas of literacy every teacher should know

To demystify talk:

● Being aware of what works in teacher talk and what doesn't: thereby talking less, giving better explanations, asking better questions, and resisting some of the clichés of teacher talk (always relying on hands up, asking closed questions, not giving thinking time, commenting on each answer).

- Understanding the difference between social, exploratory and presentational talk.

- Using a variety of groupings for structured talk – pairs, same-sex, friendship groups, by ability, by interest, random.

To demystify reading:

- Knowing how to use layout and language to make texts accessible in handouts and in presentations – e.g. white space, typographical features, summaries, bullets, short paragraphs.

- Providing assessment criteria and models of appropriate text types.

- Setting objectives for talk and providing language models – e.g. level of formality, key words and phrases.

- Using a range of strategies to support pupils' reading – e.g. reading aloud, key words and glossaries, word banks, display, paired reading, talking about texts before answering.

To demystify writing:

- Being able to write accurate, clear English, and knowing the essential ingredients in well-written prose.

- Being clear and explicit about the conventions of the writing you expect from pupils – e.g. audience, purpose, layout, key words and phrases, level of formality.

- Knowing approaches for actively teaching writing skills – such as shared composition, modelling the writing process and judicious use of writing frames.

- Knowing strategies for helping pupils to spell key words accurately and knowing how to respond to their incorrect spellings.

- Assessing pupils' work in a way that builds their competence and confidence as writers in your subject.

Literacy essentials

TALKING POINTS

- So which of these do you do most and least?
- Which do you need to learn more about?
- Which do you most strongly agree with and disagree with?

How to be effective as a literacy coordinator

Being appointed to the post of Literacy Coordinator can prove unexpectedly frustrating.

Of course, you begin, quite rightly, with a well-deserved sense of exhilaration: you have been selected for a role with whole-school significance. It's a big job that is recognised by everyone as being fundamental to the school's progress.

But the appointment of a 'coordinator' can also send out messages that literacy is someone else's job. It can make teachers assume that the teaching of skills for reading, thinking and writing is someone else's responsibility – when in fact, of course, it's the responsibility of every teacher.

So right from the outset be clear about that word 'coordinator'. It's a Latin word meaning to order or arrange things. That's important: your job is to 'join up', not to 'do everything'.

Here are ten suggestions for how to be most effective as Literacy Coordinator:

- See your role as keeping the school's eye on literacy. You're not 'doing' literacy on their behalf.

- That means identifying areas of strength and weakness (I'm trying to avoid the numbingly mechanical word 'audit' here) of current practice, and then having a simple plan of what to do over the next two to three years.

19

Literacy essentials

- A longer-term plan is more realistic than a one-year plan because literacy isn't a quick hit.

- The plan should include what the main focus is in a given half-term (e.g. looking at marking; looking at the teaching of key vocabulary; looking at reading for pleasure). It should include what different people will do, what training will take place, and what monitoring should happen. The area of focus should then recur in a later part of the plan (e.g. a year on) so that you can judge what impact has been made and what progress there has been.

- Have a small group of pupils who provide feedback on impact. Use them, for example, to look critically at every classroom: ask them 'what is there in each room that helps you to read better and write better?' 'What is there that helps you to see what standard of work is expected of you?' 'Does the room help you to speak, read and write like an expert in that subject?'

- Have a half-termly 30-minute meeting booked in with the headteacher to keep reporting on progress.

- If you have a headteacher who likes to play the pinstriped chief executive role, insist that he or she must be involved in monitoring literacy – by looking at books, talking to pupils, reading questionnaires – otherwise this most important school project won't have clout.

- Have a literacy governor who you can involve – perhaps in walking around the school with you, or talking to pupils.

- Involve other key players who can feel marginalised in schools – the librarian and teaching assistants. There's more on their roles later in this book.

- Remember that small changes can lead to big changes. Work with key players – departments and keen members of staff – to try out ideas that can then be spread more widely. Get one team trialling a 'thinking time' approach to asking better questions. Get feedback from them and pupils, then feed it into the next team. We're aiming to get literacy into the school's bloodstream and that may require a step-by-step approach rather than assuming it will all happen as a result of a one-day training session.

Literacy coordinators, more than many roles in school, need to be optimistic and persistent. Their motto might best be drawn from the advice of Winston Churchill: 'KBO'. If you don't know it, I'll leave you to Google it.

TALKING POINTS

- So how does this link with the current role of Literacy Coordinator?
- What could you be doing more of and, crucially, less of?

How a consistent whole-school approach to literacy can help pupils to learn better

Consistency across schools is one of the most difficult aspects of quality to achieve. Many of us know that from our own experience: we chose to study a subject and then to become a teacher of it because we happened to have an inspiring teacher when we were young. If we had been in the class next door, things might have been different. It's the long-standing lottery of school-life, and something that the literacy agenda – called teaching and learning – allows us to address.

Here are twenty whole-school literacy ingredients, which could have the biggest impact on helping pupils to learn:

Classrooms and corridors

● Key words for the subject are on display.

● Annotated examples of what high quality work looks like are visible.

● Displays which are readable from a distance, e.g. with questions rather than statements ('Why did Hitler rise to power?').

● The learning objective for every lesson is evident: pupils know (a) what they are expected to learn and (b) how they will demonstrate it.

How a whole-school approach can help pupils learn better

Teacher talk

- Less use of 'what?' questions and more use of 'why?' and 'how?' (this is called exploratory talk).
- Students are given time for 'oral rehearsal' – briefly discussing their answers in pairs before being expected to say them aloud.
- Students are given thinking time (e.g. 10 seconds) before giving an answer.
- Increasing use of no-hands-up.

Reading

- Teachers teach the reading skills needed in their subject – e.g. skimming (gist of a test), scanning (finding key information), analysis, speed reading and research.
- Handouts are presented in a way that is attractive and accessible, with the reading age of pupils taken account of.
- Key words are included at the start of handouts.
- Any handouts include a 'big picture' question or statement that helps pupils to understand why they are reading it.
- Questions about a text go beyond simple comprehension to explore the 'why' and 'how' of issues.

Writing

- Students see their teacher modelling how to write the first paragraph of an essay/evaluation/description, etc. This is collaborative writing and has a huge impact.
- The essential connectives of writing are taught (e.g. however, because, as, so, although, while, despite, on the other hand).
- Students are encouraged to use short sentences at the start and end of paragraphs ('This experiment was problematic.' and longer sentences in the middle 'Although we added potassium, the results still proved unexpected . . .').

Literacy essentials

Speaking and listening

● Students are asked questions based on 'how' and 'why' rather than just 'what'.

● Teachers model the kind of language they expect in group discussions and answers (key vocabulary/key connectives).

Vocabulary building

● Teachers explicitly teach the key words in their subject. Department for Education research suggests that repetition of a word four times with a clear explanation is very effective.

● Key words are given to pupils as homework, put in the planner, made into tutor time quizzes, so that they are the expected discourse of all pupils, not just those from privileged backgrounds.

TALKING POINTS
● Which of these twenty points would you say were current strengths in your classroom/department/school?
● Which are the main areas that need developing?

What Ofsted expects to see as evidence of whole-school literacy

Ofsted has given increased emphasis to literacy in the most recent incarnation of the inspection framework. Wisely – almost as if they had read this book! – they choose not to call it literacy, but instead refer to 'reading, writing and communication'. It's not an attractive phrase but it does map out the territory with some clarity.

Their guidance to inspection teams – many of whom may have little direct and recent experience of teaching reading and writing, of giving feedback, of marking books – is detailed and helpful. You can download it from the Ofsted site (www.ofsted.gov.uk).

Inspectors have the following questions to use in framing their judgements:

- Are key terms and vocabulary clear and explored with pupils to ensure that they recognise and understand them? Are they related to similar words or the root from which they are derived?

- Do teachers identify any particular features of key terms and help pupils with strategies for remembering how to spell them or why they might be capitalised (e.g. 'Parliament' in history or citizenship)?

- Do teachers remind pupils of important core skills – for example how to skim a text to extract the main elements of its content quickly or to scan a text for information about a key word or topic?

- Do teachers make expectations clear before pupils begin a task – for example on the conventions of layout in a formal letter or on the main features of writing persuasively?

- Do teachers reinforce the importance of accuracy in spoken or written language – for example, emphasising the need for correct sentence punctuation in one-sentence answers or correcting 'we was . . .' in pupils' speech?

- Do teachers identify when it is important to use standard English and when other registers or dialects may be used – for example, in a formal examination answer and when recreating dialogue as part of narrative writing?

- Do teachers help pupils with key elements of literacy as they support them in lessons? Do they point out spelling, grammar or punctuation issues as they look at work around the class?

- Does teachers' marking support key literacy points? For example, are key subject terms always checked for correct spelling? Is sentence punctuation always corrected?

TALKING POINTS

- Is the Ofsted list comprehensive? Are there other aspects of reading, writing and communication that you would expect to see?
- What are the implications of the list for your department and school?

PART TWO

Speaking and listening

Overview: what great teachers do

Great teachers use spoken language with apparently effortless skill in their classrooms.

Their own language will be vivid, clear, perhaps entertaining, and a model of the kind of language that our pupils will need if they are themselves to speak like scientists, historians, designers, musicians and so on.

Great teachers don't just teach their subject: they use and demonstrate the language of the expert. Note what that doesn't mean: it's not just about rattling off fancy vocabulary and complicated concepts in order to exude expertise: this is about teaching, not demonstrating.

Great teachers therefore do something rather more nuanced. They know that they need to give their pupils the opportunity to develop their spoken language in formal and informal contexts. They will do what is at the heart of all of our approaches: help pupils to understand and practise the skills we in the literacy club do implicitly by making those skills explicit.

Great teachers will therefore build variety into their lessons: times when they explain; times when they question; times when they expect pupils to be using exploratory talk; times when they listen to pupil explanations; times when they comment on these themselves and times when they don't.

Speaking and listening

All of this hints at the often intangible richness of the way speaking and listening underpins and enables learning in the classrooms of great teachers. It's not something we see happening often enough; but when we do, it's a privilege to be in that lesson.

Essential knowledge at a glance

This topic has two sections: pupil talk and teacher talk. Pupil talk is about how we create contexts for pupils to use language to think, express ideas, deepen their knowledge and learn social skills. Teacher talk is the way we as teachers, teaching assistants and mentors use language to help pupils in that process.

As humans, our ability to speak and listen precedes the 'taught' skills of reading and writing and their significance in the learning process can be too easily taken for granted by teachers. In fact, a classroom in which high quality learning is taking place will almost always have high quality spoken language and listening skills at its heart.

In practice this isn't just conversation skills, group work or teacher questioning. Good speaking and listening has more depth and variety to it.

Social talk in school is important. Many of our pupils from more disadvantaged backgrounds live in a context where conversation – being asked open questions and being given time to express an opinion, and space to be listened to – may be rare.

A civilised school culture can promote such skills and, to some extent, compensate for aspects of linguistic deprivation.

But social talk isn't enough to help pupils to learn better. Great teachers are adept at using and promoting 'exploratory talk' – spoken language that encourages deeper thinking.

What research tells us about classroom talk

Based at the University of Cambridge, Neil Mercer is a leading expert on classroom talk. Here he synthesises some of the key messages about the subject:

About children:

- Talk – of the right quality – promotes the development of children's reasoning, conceptual understanding and reading comprehension.
- Many children do not get a rich enough experience of spoken language outside school for this development to be assured.
- Children do not just need experience of speaking and listening in school, they need to be expressly taught the relevant functional skills: how to use talk to construct arguments, jointly solve problems and comprehend texts.

Children learn most from talk in class when:

- the teacher develops children's reflective awareness of how to talk and work together;
- the teacher encourages them to express tentative ideas;
- the teacher 'models' good talk skills in whole class discussions;
- the teacher 'scaffolds' group work but mainly stays out of it;

- group work involves tasks that really require children to 'think together'.

About teachers:

Teachers are very aware that some children lack experience and skills in using talk for thinking. However, most teachers do not expressly teach children to become better at using talk for reasoning, discussing and solving problems. If they 'teach talk', English teachers tend to focus on developing good 'presentational talk', not good 'exploratory talk'.

There are some outstanding examples of good practice in helping children develop their talk skills, which can inform training.

TALKING POINTS

- What are the implications of these findings for your own classroom, department, school?
- Do you give pupils you teach experience of exploratory talk?
- How is talk viewed in your school – by 'the management', by different subject teams, by pupils?

Exploring different types of talk

It is easy to assume that talk is talk. We see that approach in classrooms where talk happens, but often talk for the sake of talking. One of the useful functions of Neil Mercer and Steve Hodgkinson's summary of different types of talk is that we can begin to have a more nuanced approach to the way we use talk in lessons:

> *Social talk* – used to bind one to another, and to hold a group or learning community together. When pupils know and care about one another, differences can become a way of strengthening their combined power to affect change. Students can be inspired to act on behalf of one another, and for others who cannot act or speak for themselves. Students can learn the importance of learning to listen beyond the words to capture the ideas being represented.
>
> *Exploratory talk* – used to work at understanding new ideas that matter. When pupils feel comfortable with one another they can begin to explore new boundaries to their learning and to challenge one another's thinking. They can feel safe sharing 'half baked' ideas, revising their own thinking, and questioning the ideas of others.
>
> *Presentation talk* – used to share new understandings with others. When pupils reflect on what they have learned, and

consider the audience for their presentations, they can view their learning from a new perspective. Sharing with others can invite pupils to reflect on their learning.

Meta-talk – used to explore and discuss talk as an artefact. When pupils make their talk visible, they can become more aware of it and the power it can have to help them think deeply and critically . . . make their talk visible and discuss how their talk and thinking work.

Critical talk – used to invite a critique of pupils' own views and of contemporary society, the talk of critical conversations. When pupils engage in critique, they can raise questions about the way things are, dream up possibilities about the way things could be, and then inspire others to join them making changes.

From Mercer and Hodkinson,
Exploring Talk in School, Sage, 2008.

TALKING POINTS
- Does anyone at your school make such distinctions about types of talk?
- How might it be helpful to do so?
- Which forms of talk currently dominate and which are left to chance?

How to organise group talk

The default mode in our lessons and tutor time can be 'turn to your neighbour and discuss these questions'. The problem here, as we have been exploring throughout the book, is that it often reinforces existing social patterns of the word-rich and the word-poor.

We know from Dylan Wiliam's work that teachers in the UK are likely to ask more questions than teachers in the highest-performing countries and that we tend to pay less prior attention to the questions we will ask. In other words, the planning of questions is something we do less of.

I suspect it's the same, in many classrooms, with how we group pupils. The result may be that pupils fall into similar routines of 'talking to their neighbour' or interacting with the group they happen to be sitting near.

Below, from the National Strategies era, are a number of ways in which we can reinvigorate social groupings, building the groups around the intended purpose of the lesson, and providing different talk opportunities for different pupils. The groupings alone, though, aren't enough to create high quality talk. One of the key lessons about literacy is the need to make explicit the conventions and assumptions that underpin the way successful language users speak. As teachers, therefore, we should aim not just to put pupils into different groups, but then to explain and demonstrate the kind of spoken language we expect to hear. In practice that might sound like this:

> In a moment – not yet – you'll be working in your small groups and examining the question on the whiteboard. After six minutes I will ask the envoy from each group to move to the next group. Your role is to explain what your group found out. You'll use words like "we" rather than "I"; you will use words to explain such as "found out" and "discovered", and words to express opinion such as "decided" and "believe" . . .

That stage of making language expectations explicit is a really important dimension to making the grouping most effective.

Here are some examples of ways in which group interaction can be given greater variety:

Listening triads

Pupils are in groups of three – a talker, a questioner and a recorder who reports back. Note the built-in element of critical talk here: it becomes part of the rationale of the activity rather than an after-thought. It will work especially well if the pupil who takes on the 'recorder' role is briefed by the teacher beforehand, or if the group do some preliminary prediction of the kinds of words, phrases, structure and spoken features they might listen for.

Envoys

After a task, one person from each group visits another group to share ideas, then reports back to the original group.

Snowball

In pairs, pupils discuss or brainstorm ideas, then double up to fours, which then double up to eight, leading to a whole-class debate. This allows a form of 'oral rehearsal' whereby pupils can test out their ideas in a smaller, more reassuring context before speaking in front of a larger group. We know that oral rehearsal has a powerful effect on many pupils. In part it's a confidence-building device but it also builds good language habits because pupils will have time to formulate and phrase their thinking without the public element. They are more likely, as a result, to speak more reflectively, without, for example, simply deploying the first word that comes to mind.

Rainbow groups

After a separate group task, pupils are regrouped by a colour, to make new groups comprising someone from each old group.

Jigsaw

Before a task, 'home' groups allocate a section to each member. New 'expert' groups then form for each section. Finally, 'home' groups re-form* and share findings.

Spokesperson

Students discuss a topic. The idea is for the group as a whole to analyse an issue, to get a deeper understanding of it. Each spokesperson is asked in turn for a new point. If she doesn't have an immediate point to make, she has 20 seconds to consult her group. The aim is to get away from the 'I don't know' syndrome by legitimising thinking and consultation time.

Observer/listener

To develop critical talk, I recommend that no talk-based activity takes place in class without a pupil having the role of observer/ listener. Her role is to watch the group dynamic and listen to their language use. Feedback on each group's interaction and language reinforces the sense of language being used critically and reflectively.

TALKING POINTS

- In your school, do certain teachers in certain subjects excel at using groupings effectively? How are their skills harnessed?
- What role might pupils have in helping to develop a deeper culture of group talk across school: is there training that they could participate in and lead?

LANGUAGE COMMENTARY

* Notice how I've spelt 're-form'. It seems to me that here's an example of a word which benefits from a hyphen. Most writers would probably spell it as 'reform', but that has different associations – of change and refreshment; I'm using a more precise meaning of the word – 'to form again'. I think the hyphen enables the reader to get that meaning immediately rather than having to pause momentarily and reorder the semantics (in fact, I'm now thinking that 'reorder' would probably be clearer as 're-order').

Why group work matters

This summary of research evidence on group work is drawn mainly from *Effective Teaching: a Review of the Literature* by David Reynolds and Daniel Muijs (2005), used as part of the excellent National Strategies materials on 'Pedagogy and Practice'; plus the insights of Phil Beadle in his feisty handbook *How to Teach* (2010); plus my own observations.

Reason 1: It can aid learning

In most schools pupils don't do enough group work. Astonishingly, in a survey of primary schools Muijs and Reynolds found that less than 10% of lesson time was spent doing group work. Instead they are more likely to get teacher-led discussion, memorably characterised by Phil Beadle (*How to Teach*, p110) like this:

> The teacher-led discussion is merely an unthinking default setting . . . an utterly inefficient way of running a discussion as only one person is allowed to speak at a time [leaving] thirty others in a state of utter passivity or, worse still, totally zoned out.

Reason 2: It can assist pupils' social development

Putting pupils in groups is not a guarantee that they will learn more effectively: it shouldn't be seen as automatically enabling better learning or more amicable interaction. In fact, I suspect we have all seen group work that generates lots of happy activity but little that could be described as learning. It therefore needs an underpinning rationale.

Johnson and Johnson (1999) suggest that to create cooperative, purposeful groups five ingredients are required:

- positive independence, so that pupils feel that their success is built upon needing to work together;
- face-to-face supportive interaction: they should actively help one another to learn and give each other positive feedback;
- accountability – individually and as a group – for their success;
- interpersonal skills: communication, trust, leadership, decision-making and conflict-resolution;
- group-processing: a level of reflection about how they have performed as a group and what they could do to improve.

Reason 3: It can assist pupils' linguistic development

It is certainly well-documented that group work can improve pupils' social skills. It can also help their linguistic development. Using Robert K. Merton's concept of 'The Matthew Effect', which is developed by Daniel Rigney, we know that in education, as in Monopoly, the rich get richer and the poor get poorer (Rigney describes Leonard Beeghly's version of the game that gives different players different sums of money at the outset. With complete inevitability the player with most money wins. That shouldn't be a surprise: she simply buys up all the property she can and the poorest player gets into a rapid spiral of debt).

So it is with vocabulary. Department for Education research suggests that by the age of seven the gap in the vocabulary known by children in the top and bottom quartiles will be something like 4,000 words (children in the top quartile know around 7,000 words). The word-poor will never catch up because to do so they would need to be able to learn more words more quickly than the word-rich.

The best book on vocabulary generally, in my opinion, is Geoffrey Miller's provocative *The Mating Mind* (2001). It's provocative because he suggests a specific reason that 'human vocabulary size seems to have rocketed out of control': it's the necessity of attracting a mate. Our lexical variety, he suggests, is the way we impress and lure would-be partners. Size, it seems, matters.

To develop our extensive vocabulary – and Miller estimates that the average adult human speaker knows 60,000 words against the average non-speaking primate's five to twenty distinct calls – we have to start young. Between the age of eighteen months and eighteen years, human children need to learn something between ten and twenty words a day.

That's where the word-rich have the big advantage: they will hear and then read a larger range of words from an early age. Their confidence and usage will grow as a result.

That's why in schools, in all subjects, we have such a privileged opportunity to help our pupils with something that is too easily taken for granted – the chance to extend their communicative skills. Group work provides an opportunity for the word-poor to mingle with the word-rich, to hear language being used by pupils of their own age in ways that they might not otherwise encounter.

So, at the risk of being too grandiose, we mustn't forget the importance that thoughtful groupings give to the social mobility agenda.

Which brings me on to what I believe is the best educational book about vocabulary: *Bringing Words to Life* (2002) by three US academics, Isabel L. Beck, Margaret G. McKeown and Linda Kucan (what is it with Americans including the initials from their middle names, by the way?)*. They provide compelling evidence for the social impact of vocabulary – such as 'high school seniors near the top of their class [knowing] about four times as many words as their low-performing classmates'. (p1).

We have to do something about this. We have a responsibility.

TALKING POINTS

- All this talk of the word-poor and the word-rich: does it convince you? Do you see it as part of your responsibility to address such issues?
- How might the 'social' times of the school day – tutor time, breaks, extra-curricular sessions – be used to reinforce the benefits of different pupil groupings?

LANGUAGE COMMENTARY

*Purists will accuse me of being ungrammatical here because I start a sentence emphatically with 'Which'. I think it works but it might antagonise the grammar police. 'Which' is usually used within a sentence to link ideas ('I'm looking forward to the holiday which we finally booked last night'). That's how I'm using it – but I've used the word at the start of a sentence, rather as I might use 'that'. It's not truly grammatical: but I think you'll see what I'm doing and why I'm doing it.

Why body language matters so much in teaching

It is easy and deceptive to assume that great teachers are essentially human repositories of knowledge – that subject knowledge is all that counts. In reality, I suspect we have all been taught by really clever teachers who turn out to be rubbish at teaching. Knowledge isn't enough.

Add to that the fact that our pupils have an unerring ability to judge whether we are any good before there's chance to demonstrate whether we know our stuff or not, and it leads us into an area of school life that isn't much discussed in teacher training – and which I think ought to be.

This is a good example of where my definition of literacy is taking us beyond what many readers might expect. A very powerful bit of research (quoted below) suggests that pupils will know with remorseless accuracy whether we are any good as teachers long before we open our mouths. Our body language – the stuff we rarely think about, let alone get trained in – shapes the way we are judged.

So this chapter – as with all of our work on literacy – tries to take the implicit and to make it explicit.

First, the theory. In his book *Blink: The Power of Thinking Without Thinking*, the writer Malcolm Gladwell (2006) describes an experiment in which American pupils are asked to rate the quality of a teacher. What makes the experiment particularly interesting is that the teachers were on video with the sound turned down.

Here's how Gladwell describes it:

> How long did it take you, when you were in college, to decide how good a teacher your professor was? A class? Two classes? A semester? The psychologist Nalini Ambady once gave pupils three ten-second videotapes of a teacher – with the sound turned off – and found they had no difficulty at all coming up with a rating of the teacher's effectiveness. Then Amabady cut the clips back to five seconds, and the ratings were the same. They were remarkably consistent even when she showed the pupils just two seconds of videotape. Then Ambady compared those snap judgements of teacher effectiveness with evaluations of those same professors made by their pupils after a full semester of classes, and she found that they were also essentially the same. The person watching a silent two-second video clip of a teacher he or she has never met will reach conclusions about how good that teacher is that are very similar to those of a pupil who has sat in the teacher's class for an entire semester. That's the power of our adaptive unconscious.
>
> (pp.12–13)

This has powerful implications for the way we work as teachers and for the way we train new recruits to our profession. These first impressions aren't being arrived at purely in response to our use of language: it's our body language, the way in which we stand, where we decide to stand, how we demonstrate that the territory of the classroom belongs to us.

As with literacy, the best veteran teachers know much of this intuitively. Great teaching is often a matter of taking the implicit (how we read a demanding text, how we write in a technical style) and making it explicit to our pupils.

In this section I want to do something similar with the body language used by teachers to establish their authority and credibility.

Speaking and listening

TALKING POINTS

- From your own memories of being taught and from more recent observations, what immediately strike you as the essential aspects of body language that great teachers deploy?
- What are your own body language mannerisms – where do you position yourself in the room? Do you stand or sit? How do you get a class to stop talking? What verbal mannerisms are you aware of?

How to enter the classroom

This heading will strike some readers as bizarre. Are we really devoting a page of a book about literacy to explaining how to enter a classroom? The answer, of course, is yes and the reason will be clear if you read the introduction to this section. First impressions matter, and they matter especially in teaching where a blend of authority and credibility are essential ingredients in being successful.

In the past teachers were regularly expected to cover for absent colleagues. Nothing quite tested your core classroom skills like this. You would turn up to a class you didn't know studying a subject you didn't know in a room you didn't know. Many of us earned our stripes in this way.

In an ideal world we should aim to be at the classroom before the class. That's important symbolically because it means that the pupils are entering our territory and we can set the tone. The way we greet them at the door, our expectations of how they enter, the way the room has been prepared, the desks arranged – all of these carry a message about our values, about what we believe in and what we will require of our pupils.

Some schools formalise this. They have a 'house style' whereby all pupils are expected to line up outside a classroom and all teachers required to have a seating plan which (for example) sits boy beside girl in alphabetical order.

Speaking and listening

I don't subscribe to that approach, but there's no doubt that it can make life easier for new teachers and cover supervisors. It means that part of the process of establish authority, of wanting to insist that the territory of the classroom is yours, has been done for you.

Routines and systems such as this can be easily sneered at, but in fact they support less confident teachers by signalling to pupils that a teacher's authority – whether new to the school or a seasoned veteran of many years – is a consistent value across the school.

So you'll want to know before you start at a new school whether such systems are in place.

Let's assume that they aren't. Let's also assume that, for one reason or another, you haven't been able to get to the classroom ahead of the group you're about to teach. They're in the room waiting for you and that walk to the lesson is likely to be one that fills you with disquiet or even dread. Even the most battle-scarred teachers of the country's toughest schools will admit that nerves continue to play a part in their lives, just as they do in the bodies of great actors.

This is where the symbolism of teaching is so important and so different from belonging to other professions. I'm not sure an accountant, for example, needs to learn how to play the part of an accountant, or needs guidance in opening the office door.

But that's what makes teaching such a rewarding career (if you're cut out for it) and so seemingly difficult in the early days to get right.

So: back to how to open the classroom door. To counter any butterflies, that walk across to the room will need a psychological ploy of some kind. You'll have to take deep breaths, or count, or concentrate your energy into walking confidently, looking around, making eye-contact, smiling, saying thank you to pupils who hold doors open . . . that kind of thing.

Then, once you get to the room you will be teaching in, the trick is to open the door very confidently. Show that you belong here, that you know this place (even if you don't). Demonstrating authority is now done largely through symbolic gestures. Show that you are taking command of the territory. Change the lights, flicking a switch to show that you're commanding the ambience (whether adding light or making the room darker doesn't matter – this is all symbolism, remember).

Bear in mind also Phil Beadle's handy dictum that a lesson will never be any good if pupils are wearing coats and have bags on desks. So immediately, with calm purpose, set about reining in the group. Put your own books and papers on the teacher's desk, then stand in front of the class and begin to take command. Pay attention to the environment – change it to show that you are in command. Here are the kinds of utterances you might use:

> Could you just open that window there slightly for me? Thank you.

> Morning everyone. Bags quickly on the floor, planners and pens on desks, coats off. Thanks very much. Let's get going.

That use of 'thank you' is important. Whereas 'please' carries an inevitable sense of pleading, 'thank you' conveys greater authority: it implies an expectation that what you are requesting will be done. It turns a request into an assumed action: 'Could you pick up that piece of litter for me: thank you.'

And so you're perhaps 10 seconds in and, if Gladwell's quoted research is right, then the class will have made their judgement about you. You want to have created a first impression of purpose, calm authority, a sense that you know what you're doing and that you mean business.

If you're still training to teach, or just considering it, watch a teacher at work in this initial stage of a lesson. Try to be there before he or she arrives and watch for the symbolic gesture, the way the implicit message is reinforced: 'this is my territory and I'm in charge'.

Speaking and listening

TALKING POINTS

● Sound advice? Which parts do you agree or disagree with?
● How might this topic be built into the training and induction of new teachers in your school or department?

How to use the classroom space

Where we stand as teachers is important. Every class will have its zones where the more compliant pupils choose to sit (usually nearer the front and in direct sightlines with you), while the more disruptive will choose to sit at desks towards the back and probably at the side of the room.

Once we know these rules of engagement, it's far easier to feel as teachers that we are in authority – that we will redefine the rules.

That's why early on you are well advised to implement a seating plan. If your school has this as a policy, it will be much easier to enforce. Students will arrive at your first lesson expecting to be told where they will be sitting.

But, if that's not the case, then this is your classroom and your subject and you should make it one of your opening expectations that there will be a rationale for seating.

Some teachers get very hooked up on how this rationale should work – boy/girl combinations, arranged alphabetically seem especially voguish. I'm not quite convinced by the gender dimension there, with its subtext that girls are being used to mollify the effects of the boys, to 'civilise' them.

Some expert teachers, such as Phil Beadle, point to the fact that since pupils will learn better in groups, your classroom should be set out to encourage collaboration. Again, I'm leaving that to you. All I know is that first impressions count and you need therefore to establish your own authority in a light-touch but effective way within the first ten seconds. A seating plan will help.

It may be that in the corridor, before pupils enter, you say something like this:

> Good morning, everyone. My name's Mr Barton and I'm looking forward to teaching you English this year. I do have a seating plan for today's lesson and so want you to listen for your name and then to come into the classroom and sit where I ask you. That will allow me to get to see how you work together and make sure we have a really successful year. So coats off and then I'll start bringing you in.

Acknowledging that transcriptions such as this will often feel stilted on the page, this set of instructions does the job. It's clear and purposeful and positive.

You would then want to stand at the door and call pupils' names. As they come to the door you would probably say something like 'Hello, so you're Ashley: just over there please at that desk . . .'

Again, the tone is positive and purposeful. And it may be that your seating plan is alphabetically boy/girl, or purely alphabetical, or done by star signs. The point about seating plans is that they are part of the symbolism of the classroom – as significant as asking a pupil to turn down the radiator temperature or open a window: they signify that the territory of the classroom is ours.

That's why I'm inclined to keep refreshing seating plans, to keep pupils on their toes, to change who sits by whom. I was taught by a very inspiring and vaguely menacing teacher whose motto could have been 'expect the unexpected'.

I'd want to make this part of my repertoire, changing the rationale for seating with unexpected regularity, so that pupils get to sit with and work with a full range of others. In literacy terms, as we shall see when we encounter 'The Matthew Effect' later, this is more important than it seems.

TALKING POINTS

- Which elements of this do you agree with and disagree with?
- How does it relate to your own teaching? Do you have certain habits – such as places where you always stand and sit? How might you refresh your repertoire as a result?

How to avoid letting no-go zones develop in your classroom

This topic will strike some readers as odd. To others – from school days or training or current experience – it will be all too chillingly familiar.

As teachers we can quickly solidify into certain habits. We might, for example, develop verbal traits that become a source of amusement or irritation to our pupils or colleagues. Words and phrases such as 'okay' and 'you know' can quickly shift from being friendly requests for feedback to linguistic ticks that are used to define or lampoon us. More on this later.

But the same principle applies to how we use the classroom space. We can easily fall into routines whereby we always teach from the same spot in the room, giving our lessons a kind of predictability. That's when, with some classes, no-go-zones can develop – areas of the classroom where pupils intent on being disruptive may feel that they are in the ascendancy. That's why it's important to continually refresh the seating plan, and to be bold about this, not bowing to pupil requests to leave things as they are.

But there are other important steps too to make sure that the whole territory of the classroom remains symbolically yours. Key to this is being seen to teach from different and perhaps unexpected parts of the classroom. This is especially useful if you're reading something aloud and need pupils to follow along. Stand at the back of the room, behind the pupils, so that they aren't sure who you're looking at.

On other occasions, use displays in the room – e.g. of key words – and go and stand by the display, drawing attention to the words pupils should try to incorporate into their spoken or written responses.

All of this is a simple reminder of the symbolism of the classroom, that where you stand matters as much as how you stand, and it will ensure that no-go-zones are unlikely to develop.

TALKING POINTS

- What's your experience of teaching a group where a small core made the lessons difficult?
- Where did they sit? How did you deal with them? What would you do differently now?

Where and how to stand in class

Remember that this book is chiefly about opinion, not advice. You'll pick and choose the parts you agree with and disregard the other bits as the gibbering rants of a pompous old fool. So, with that disclaimer neatly out of the way, here goes. Great teachers teach standing up. There.

I rarely see good teaching if the teacher is sitting down. I don't mean when teaching an A-level group, seminar-style. I mean teaching a class of twenty eight or so Year 9 pupils. Sitting down reduces the teacher's authority and implies an informality, a casualness, which we may delude ourselves is a sign of our excellent relationship with a class but, in my experience, is rarely that.

The weakest teachers will open the door to the classroom with an air of unspoken timidity, move across the room, and stand too far back from the class, possibly with a desk in front of him. He will exude anxiety and might as well wear a badge saying 'victim'.

Where and how we stand matters rather a lot. The getting to the standing position – that is, opening the door and walking across the room, needs to be done with a kind of brazen confidence. It's like so often in teaching: you have to bluff it, pretending you know more than you do or that you're more self-assured than you really are. The ability to play the part of teacher is essential.

So if the class is already in the room, open the door and walk in with confidence. Put your things on the desk and begin the symbolic process of signalling that the territory is now yours. Ask for all bags off desks, for planners, books and pens to be out in front of pupils, for coats to be off. This is the inevitable routine of most lesson starts.

Go a step further to show that this is now your domain: ask a pupil to open a window slightly or close a window slightly. Ask another to adjust the heating. Ask another to straighten a poster at the back of the room. Walk to the light switch and switch one light on or off. Do anything, in other words, that signals 'under new management', that demonstrates that you have arrived. This is the dark symbolism of the classroom.

Then stand in front of the class, a little closer to the pupils at the front of the room than they might expect. It's a kind of 'invasion of body space' approach. Show that you mean business and that no no-go zones will be developing in your classroom. Just stand there and drive the silence that you expect by standing still, looking at pupils, using any gestures to accompany you saying 'Thank you, pens and books down, turning around this way so that we can start. Thanks very much.'

If the class are noisy, or they aren't paying attention, don't raise your voice. Have an object – a board rubber or set of keys or something – which you can use to tap firmly on the desk to get attention. Personally, I get inordinate pleasure from doing this so loudly that a pupil usually yelps in shock at the noise; but I'm not recommending it: you'll want to find your own method of grabbing attention. The main thing is: don't shout for quiet. It's contradictory and a bit demeaning.

My point is that signalling that you're now commanding the room is an essential part of a lesson sequence. Choose the right place at the front and make this your regular starting space, at least for the first few lessons with a group. In later lessons you may want to surprise pupils by standing somewhere else – such as at the back of the room – but in these early stages, routines matter.

Speaking and listening

TALKING POINTS

- Do you agree with the premise about signalling that as teacher you have taken command of the territory?
- What do you do when entering a classroom where the pupils are already waiting? How do you establish yourself? Where do you stand? How do you bring the class to silent attention?

How other aspects of body language can help to improve your communication

The 'don't smile until Christmas' advice is something that some teachers continue to use. The idea seems to be that keeping a stern aspect and being a stickler for classroom rules for a long period establishes your authority. That may well work for some, but in general we have to find a style that allows us to show our personality.

After all, if we're competing with Google then one of the advantages we have is that we can interact with pupils. And remembering the lesson of Malcolm Gladwell's *Blink* (whereby pupils will make an accurate judgement about our teaching quality long before we start teaching them), we need to use other aspects of body language to engage the group's attention and covertly establish our authority.

Stand still

The previous section looked at where and how to stand. One other piece of advice: stand still. This builds authority and avoids distracting pupils. There will always be charismatic teachers who strut around the room while firing off a volley of explanations, but, as a general rule, stay put. Allow the focus to be on what you are saying rather than where you are in the room.

Use silence

Anyone who trains teachers will confirm that one of the warning signs that all will not be well with a new teacher's discipline is a lack of authoritative silence. It's too easy and tempting when we begin teaching not to absolutely insist on complete silence. It's an essential trigger in signalling to the class that this teacher has authority. It's best gained not just by saying 'stop talking' but having a set of cues that mean it's your time as the teacher to talk. That's why most effective teachers will insist on pupils putting their pens down.

'Pens down' is, when we think about it, a slightly odd injunction to pupils. We know from our own experience that humans are perfectly capable of listening to someone talking and holding a pen. But it's another of those symbolic cues we use. 'Pens down' means 'stop talking and look this way and listen'. And it's the most important way you have of demonstrating your authority in a way which is non-confrontational and familiar to pupils.

And even though it will sometimes feel a little unnatural, both insist on silence and when you've got it, let it brew for a second: allow the silence to emphasise itself. This, again, reinforces your authority, that you insist on silence, get it, and only begin to talk when you are ready to do so.

Read aloud from the right location

Reading aloud is really important. It's something all teachers should do because it helps pupils to hear the rhythms of our language and to see how as readers we use punctuation to interpret a text.

Some teachers ask pupils to read a text aloud – for example, reading a document around the class paragraph by paragraph. I never do this. It's disjoined and creates a lot of stress for some pupils. I wouldn't want to read aloud myself in front of people if I hadn't been given time to prepare.

It's also ineffective, as pupils will sit there wondering whether it's their turn to read next and trying to guess where their 'bit' begins rather than paying attention to what's being read.

So, no: unless it's a play, or pupils are reading the characters in a story, or they are in small groups with time for preparing, let's avoid asking pupils to read aloud in class. Instead, you do it.

And, unless it's a very short passage, read from a strategically different part of the room. Personally, I would always read aloud from the back of the class. That way, pupils can't see me but I can see that they are paying attention. They are more likely to concentrate with me choosing to read aloud from the back.

To make the reading more effective, I would also usually signal beforehand that I will pause occasionally to give pupils time to reflect on what they have just read and heard. I'd try to make this sequence of the lesson calm, purposeful and slow – with the text read at a pace that allows pupils to process the information or story.

Use gestures

Gestures can give us authority too. The trouble is we rarely watch ourselves teaching – it's too excruciating – so we can fall into patterns of using gestures that don't actually help communicate our meaning. It's so easy and discreet to be able to film ourselves using a flip cam or laptop that we probably ought to do it more.

Gestures can add authority. If you are someone who is short or whose voice is quiet, gestures which involve using the arms and hands when we are explaining, make us seem bigger (I know this sounds silly: trust me). When we are using commands – for example setting up for pupils to move to one part of the room to another – gestures accompanying our words can clarify ('So in a second, when I ask you, I want to see this group here moving to this table here . . .').

Gestures can add emphasis when we are explaining concepts. They can inject a sense of vitality into a description of a process. The aim should be to use authoritative rather than either weak or aggressive gestures – clear arm movements, rhetorical flourishes, pointing, using an upturned palm for emphasis to reinforce what we are saying.

Use eye-contact

My old English teacher, Roy Samson, advised me to stand at the door as pupils arrived, to let them in and to stare at them. It was a bit like establishing with dogs who was in charge. I suspect he may have overstated the case, but there's no doubt that eye-contact matters a lot in the classroom. In particular this means looking pupils in the eye, scanning the room constantly, and using eye-contact, with a strategic pause, if someone talks when you are. In many cases this combination of a glance and a silence will be all that is needed to rein a talkative pupil in.

Use your voice

Actors often express surprise that teachers don't receive more professional voice coaching. After all, it's the main way that we communicate ideas and interact with pupils. Here are my suggestions for the essential ingredients in effective teacher talk:

A great teacher . . .

- waits before speaking: silence builds authority;
- avoids repetition of fillers ('okay', 'know what I mean', 'right');
- is clearly audible but varies volume to create texture: some bits loud, some bits quiet;
- uses pupils' names a lot: it personalises teaching;
- says 'thank you' more than 'please': it is built on the assumption that what you ask for will be done rather than pleading for it;
- doesn't talk too much;
- has alternatives to asking questions;

How body language can help improve your communication

- asks 'why?' and 'how?' questions more than 'what?';

- gives pupils thinking time before expecting answers;

- praises hugely and in a varied way – 'well done', 'nice one', 'great idea', 'fabulous', 'I hadn't thought of that'.

None of this happens by accident. It needs practice and feedback.

TALKING POINTS

- Do you agree with the list: is this what great teachers do?
- Which are the areas of strength and weakness in your own teaching?

How to talk less

As teachers, we often talk too much. Our classrooms are too often dominated by our own instructions, explanations and questions, and we are probably unaware of quite how much of an average lesson these activities might fill.

That's not to say that teachers talking is always a bad thing. We don't have to subscribe to the idea of teachers as mere 'facilitators' and expect us to look on silently from the sidelines. After all, if I have a degree in a subject and am an expert in something that my pupils need to know about, then there will be times when I should proudly and without guilt explain the topic to them.

The trouble is that we do that, and ask questions, and comment on pupils' answers so much that when shown the video evidence of our input it can reduce us to embarrassed disbelief.

We need therefore a judicious sense of self-knowledge about how we talk – knowing when and how to speak, and when not to. So that's our first rule of better teacher talk: let's talk less so that the talk we do use is more effective.

That means thinking about and planning in advance what our key messages are. It means finding ways of expressing these ideas that are simple, accessible and memorable. It may mean using language more evocatively to paint pictures with words. It may mean saying less with the spoken word but having on a whiteboard an image or a set of instructions to which we direct pupils and then leave them to refer back to.

But the main thing it means is talking less. And often (in my experience) that proves a healthy discipline: it makes us think more in advance of what we need to say.

TALKING POINTS

- How much do you talk in an average lesson? Have you recorded yourself? Have you dared to ask pupils for their feedback?
- What are the implications of this chapter for your own practice?

How to use language to manage transitions within lessons

One of the features of the talk used by great teachers is that they are quite redundant in their use of language. This means that they make judicious use of repetition. This works in various ways and, in the toolkit of a great teacher, becomes an almost imperceptible feature of their style.

First, as the great Michael Marland reminded us in his seminal book *The Craft of the Classroom* (1975), redundancy means making instructions very clear. He taught us to borrow the speaking formulation favoured by the clergy: 'Tell them what you're going to tell them; tell them; then tell them what you've told them.'

Never is this more important than when managing the transition-points in lessons. These are when you are moving from one activity to another and, in my experience, can prove the messiest part of a lesson. If I hear a pupil saying over general hubbub 'What do we have to do again, sir?' then I know that the transition arrangements weren't explained with sufficient clarity or explicitness.

Here's an example. Let's say that pupils have been introduced to a controversial topic – such as whether use of animals in laboratory testing is necessarily cruel. They have been given an introduction to the topic and are now going to discuss it in groups that the teacher has chosen. In the hands of an inexperienced teacher, this transition from plenary to group work can be a mess. The risk is that as soon as the teacher says 'Right, time to get into groups', the class starts moving and any further instructions are drowned out.

That's why heavy use of linguistic redundancy – while it looks odd on the page – helps to bring clarity and order to an important point in the lesson. It might look like this:

> We're going to finish the class discussion there because in a second I'm going to be asking you to debate some questions in a smaller group. I'm going to show you what the groups are and how I have decided them. Then I'll tell you where each group will be working and what I expect you to do. Then we'll quickly and quietly move into the groups. So, first, let's show you what the groups are.

Teacher talk like this carries lots of important signals. It's essentially using words to signal the future tense ('we're going to') and connectives, which reinforce the sense that these are instructions about what will happen in the future ('in a second'). The talk is heavily structured with connectives such as 'then' and 'first'). All of this brings a reassuring sense of clarity to the instructions and makes it more likely that even the most exuberant class will be able to manage the transition from one activity to another with relative calm.

How to explain things more clearly

When we watch great teachers of, say, History or Physics at work, they have an ability to take complex concepts and make them easy to understand. For many of us, that's the true mark of a great teacher – a skill that's even more important than subject knowledge: it's about communication.

The key ingredients in explaining clearly might include:

- Telling pupils what you're going to tell them – giving them some kind of 'big picture' or the relevance of what you're going to say.

- Being deliberately repetitive to emphasise key points.

- Building a sense of structure into what we say.

- Using metaphor to help pupils to visualise an abstract concept.

- Using vocabulary of different complexity within a sentence to extend pupils' understanding.

Example

Here's an example from a Year 11 Art lesson:

> I'm going to explain to you why Caravaggio's paintings created such a shock when people first saw them around 1600. I want

you to understand why these people were so upset, offended and even outraged by his work.

To understand that, you'll first need to see what religious paintings had been like before he got noticed. I'll show you a few of those paintings and frescos first (remember – frescoes are paintings done directly onto walls, usually in churches and chapels). Once we've looked at those background works of art, we'll then try to look through the eyes of people at the time at Caravaggio's early paintings.

Hopefully you will see why his work was like a bomb going off in the world of Italian art. Nothing would ever be the same again. The world was turned upside down. Let's have a look . . .

Analysis

Here's what gives clarity to the explanation:

- It begins with a statement of its purpose: 'I'm going to explain to you why . . .'. It outlines what the teacher wants from her pupils: 'I want you to understand . . .'.
- It uses connectives to help pupils to understand the way the subject is being framed: 'first', 'before', 'once', 'then'.
- It uses pronouns such as 'that' to refer back to an earlier point.
- It deploys images to help pupils to visualise the concept: 'bomb going off', 'the world turned upside down'.
- It provides a light-touch explanation of a technical term ('frescoes').

This kind of example can, of course, seem stilted and artificial when transcribed in inky letters on the page like this. Fair enough. But it's an example of the way teacher training and professional development could perhaps take more account of the way language can shape pupil learning.

Speaking and listening

After all, it's not enough to know a lot about Renaissance art: it's how far to simplify, clarify, and describe when giving an explanation to pupils.

There's a grammatical point worth making too. When we speak, both in conversation and in presentations, we often link our ideas with 'and'. We say things like:

> Today we're going to watch a short clip of people talking about the early days of the Second World War and we'll hear all their views and then we'll think about what those views tell us about the experience of being in the war and consider whether all of the people are reliable as historical witnesses . . .

In conversation this is rarely a problem. But in explanations, listeners are often helped if we more clearly signal the structure and organise ideas into self-standing sentences. It's essentially the advice the clergy used to be given about their sermons: 'Tell them what you're going to say, say it, tell them what you told them.' This means more explicitly flagging our points and speaking in shorter sentences:

> Today we'll watch a short clip of people talking about World War II. You'll see ordinary people describing their memories of the war. We'll watch it and then discuss what they say. Then I'm going to ask you as historians to decide whether their descriptions are all reliable, whether we can trust their accounts. So first we'll watch and listen; then we'll reflect on what they say. Any questions?

Use of connectives such as 'then', 'first', 'after' add a structure to the teacher's explanation. The shorter sentences reinforce the sense of clarity.

How to make explanations more powerful

There are some obvious ways that we can make our explanation of complex ideas and concepts simpler:

- Structuring what we say so that it has a logical order.
- Identifying and making explicit the key points we want pupils to learn.
- Hooking pupils' interest with an attention-grabbing opening line ('By the end of this lesson you'll be an expert in knowing how mushrooms have sex').
- Linking the topic to pupils' prior knowledge or experience.
- Using connectives to clearly signpost the content ('another', 'later', 'first').
- Using examples to illuminate a concept.
- Using props or visual aids.
- Using questions judiciously to test pupils' understanding.
- Being linguistically redundant – deliberately repeating some key concepts and vocabulary.
- Using humour to keep pupils engaged.

That's all pretty commonsensical, I suspect. But great teachers use another aspect of language to make concepts vivid. They use metaphor and analogy. This sounds more technical than it is, so don't turn the page yet.

I suspect it's something that none of us ever had mentioned in our teacher training, and yet it's a fundamental part of not just the texts we read but of the way great teachers teach.

The ability to explain with clarity and precision and appropriate brevity is one of the most important linguistic skills teachers need. And metaphor assists in that process.

Metaphor is a Greek word meaning, in its original sense, 'carry over'. You can see removal vans in Athens, for example, with the company name of Metaphor. We use the term now to illuminate one idea with an image or picture from another. According to James Geary in his brilliant book *I is an Other* (2011) 'we utter about one metaphor for every ten to twenty-five words, or about six metaphors a minute'. This will sound extraordinary and unbelievable to many people, but look at the example he gives:

> Perth is in the grip of a heat wave with temperatures set to soar to 40 degrees Celsius by the end of the week. Australia is no stranger to extreme weather. Melbourne was pummelled with hailstones the size of golf balls on Saturday. Long term, droughts, bushfires and floods have all plagued large swathes of Queensland, New South Wales and Victoria.
>
> (p.5)

The metaphors help to express the ideas more powerfully, though some have become so familiar to us that they will no longer strike us as metaphors (they are therefore 'dead' metaphors):

- in the grip
- heat wave
- to soar
- end of the week
- no stranger

- pummelled with hailstones
- plagued
- swathes

The main effect of the metaphors is to add a kind of visual immediacy, a drama. In class, metaphors help us to explain ideas. We can take a concept and describe it as if it was something else – something that helps pupils to visualise the concept.

We might describe the human eye as if it was a camera; the brain as a computer hard drive; sound waves as ripples on a pond; bird migration like a family vacation.

The secondary topic – the analogy – allows us to explore similarities and differences. Often it will help us to make a concept more tangible. Here's an example of the way I use metaphor to explain to pupils how to use the colon (the punctuation mark, not part of the large intestine):

> Colons are like car headlights: they point ahead, telling us to expect something. So as soon as you see a sentence like this, the headlights remind you to expect more:
>
> There are several reasons that Shakespeare makes Lady Macbeth disappear from the play: the first . . .
>
> Colons are therefore useful at the start of lists. They point ahead to what's next. But they work in other kinds of writing too, such as stories and articles. Look at the way you get halfway through this sentence and the headlights of the colon tell you there's more, a kind of punchline:
>
> Rich, powerful, sometimes media-obsessed and sometimes media-phobic: what is it we love about premiership footballers?
>
> The list builds up; the colon tells us there's more; the question finishes off my meaning. It's a sign of the way good use of punctuation is designed to help the reader. In this case the colon – pointing forward like headlights on a car – tells us to expect stay alert. There's something ahead.

Speaking and listening

Here are some further examples from colleagues at school, explaining ways they use metaphor in Music, Chemistry and Biology:

Chemistry (from David Thompson)

We explain the displacement of metals from a compound using the displacement disco. Copper arrives at the disco with his girlfriend oxygen, but magnesium is also there. Magnesium is a more reactive metal (I usually say that he is a super-attractive boy like Justin Bieber, to a chorus of groans) and oxygen leaves copper, and joins with magnesium. Magnesium has displaced copper from its compound.

We also explain solubility in terms of relationships. Teenagers are obsessed with relationships.

Music (from Jennie Francis and Zoe Maclachlan)

How about a perfect cadence? People often say that this is like a musical full stop. It is – but it's easier to hear if you listen for the point at which it would be fine to get up from your piano, take a bow and leave the room.

Diatonic – means through the tonic – in other words all of the notes in a passage belong to the 'home' key. Dia in this instance comes from the same place as diagonal and diarrhoea... easy to remember the through bit when you associate it with those words.

When discussing the lives of slaves I clear out the room, close the blinds and turn off the lights. I ask the students to sit in a circle around a small pile of red objects which serves as a camp fire. We visualise the fencing around us and the stars in the sky above us. I talk about my experiences that day (indignities, hard-labour, pains, sadness etc) and then introduce singing. Later on in the lesson I have them all lying on their backs (heads in the middle, although not too close to the campfire as it chucks out a lot of heat) and by that time I have got them singing in a scat style (quite quietly) whilst I accompany them on the guitar. They are all looking up at the stars and thinking about loved ones back home etc, and so are less concerned than normal about who is listening to them sing. Occasionally, we have to throw a shoe on the campfire if it looks like it needs more wood.

Biology (from Crawford Kingsnorth)

When we are talking about how a catalyst works the students often find it difficult to understand how the enzyme speeds up a chemical reaction. The biology is:

- An enzyme is a biological catalyst.

- It speeds up a chemical reaction.

- You start with the substrate. You produce the product.

- If you have two substrates they can only react when they collide (a 'successful collision').

- The enzyme provides a place for the reaction to occur, the active site.

So . . . how does providing a place for the substrates to meet speed up the reaction?

Imagine a family in a supermarket. If a child is lost, the family can spend all day walking up and down the aisles but they have to collide/meet to be reunited.

If the supermarket provides a place for people to meet customer services (similar to the enzymes' active site), and if all concerned know that if someone is lost everyone should go to customer services, the time taken to collide will be shorter.

The parents then hold the hands of the child (parent-child complex); in biology when the enzyme and substrate collide they form an enzyme-substrate complex.

Once collided the family can react: 'How many times have I told you before about wandering off, if ever you do that again you will be standing in the naughty corner for the rest of your life', etc.

Speaking and listening

Business Studies (from Penny Quintero Hunt)

Quite an old cliché but I refer to cash (as opposed to profit) in a business as the oil that keeps machinery (or sometimes I use an old bicycle) running; if the oil dries up then the machinery stops working, not because it isn't any good, it still has value (which is capital tied up in assets), but because there is nothing to keep it moving (i.e. selling/producing/paying bills) it ceases to function (i.e. administration).

TALKING POINTS

- What are the main topics you have to explain?
- Which do pupils struggle most to understand, and why?
- What kinds of metaphors and analogies do members of your subject team use to help to illuminate topics in your subject, by drawing attention to similarities and differences? Have you shared them at meetings?

How to ask better questions

Asking questions has always been an essential part of what teachers do. That's part of the problem, because there's evidence (the ubiquitous Dylan Wiliam again) to suggest that teachers in the UK ask far more questions than in many high-performing parts of the world, and that our questions aren't as good.

According to Wiliam, teachers in, say, Japan will spend less time marking pupils' books and more time planning the questions that will probe pupils' learning. They ask fewer and better questions.

My own experience confirms this. Teachers ask lots of closed questions ('What is the process called by which plants make food'), rely on hands-up, and rarely give thinking time. The main problems in questioning are:

- Not being clear why the question is being asked – a bit of a sense that this is what teachers are supposed to do.
- Asking closed questions that require short answers.
- Piling questions up so that they become confusing.
- Launching in to difficult questions without building towards them.
- Using a scattergun approach – lots of questions answered by various pupils around the room, creating a feeling of randomness.
- Accepting the first answer that's given and then moving on.

Speaking and listening

- Asking questions where essentially pupils are playing 'guess what's in the teacher's mind'.

- Not involving the whole class.

- Being afraid of showing when an answer is wrong and using it to clarify a subject for the whole class. We tend to fear damaging a child's self-esteem by showing how an answer is incorrect.

Creating a context for better questioning:

- Emphasise the classroom as a place for exploring ideas, for improving our collective understanding and where making mistakes is a natural part of learning. That, I suggest, should mean giving less superficial praise for answers and instead exploring the content of what is said.

- Use a no-hands-up approach. This depends on good discipline but can lead to a very different dynamic in the classroom. It needs deliberate flagging in the way you set up a question, like this:

   I want you in pairs to think of three reasons that the Cold War ended. Three. Be ready to explain them. You've got two minutes with your partner to come up with your three reasons. Then I'm going to choose someone to tell the class. We'll all listen and I will then ask one person to say which of those reasons you think is the main one – the most important one. Do you see?

Once again, although slightly artificial on the page, the extract shows how clarity arises from linguistic redundancy – from a heavy use of repetition.

Notice also how the need for active listening is brought to the fore by the no-hands-up rule. Pupils will need to listen because they know that they might be asked to comment. And since our purpose is to understand ideas, when you get to the part where pupils have to say which is most/least important, try to avoid evaluating it. Don't say 'very good'. Instead say 'thank you' and ask another pupil to give her response; then another. Then ask another pupil which of the three responses she most agrees with.

● Always build in thinking time and oral rehearsal. This isn't making questioning 'easier'; it's not a dilution. Rather, it's a way of developing more thoughtful responses and making it more likely that a pupil who lacks confidence will respond because she has had the opportunity to rehearse her answer with a partner or in a small group.

● To develop more extended responses, ask 'why' and 'how' questions and tell pupils that their answers must contain more than, say, twenty words.

● To avoid the scattergun approach, use an interrogation technique. Signal in advance that you are going to give pupils time to revise a topic. Then you're going to choose one of them and you – or a pupil – will interrogate what she knows. If she gets stuck, then she just needs to ask others in the group to help her out. This approach – so long as you choose the right pupil! – allows knowledge to be explored in more detail because we're not having to retune into a range of different voices around the room.

There are, of course, alternatives to questions, and in the reading section – where there can be a default mode of giving pupils a text followed by a set of questions, we explore some of the alternatives to using a string of questions.

TALKING POINTS

● Is your own classroom characterised by questions? Do you plan questions?
● Which techniques in this chapter do you already use? Which might you try out?
● What work is done in your school on training teachers to ask better questions? What could be done?

PART THREE

Reading

Introduction

The more we think about it, the more extraordinary the human invention of reading is. As scholar and bibliophile Alberto Manguel says in his compelling book *The History of Reading* (1997):

> I could perhaps live without writing. I don't think I could live without reading. Reading – I discovered – comes before writing. A society can exist – many do – without writing, but no society can exist without reading.
>
> (p.7)

While some may dispute his assumption that a purely oral culture cannot count as a 'society', there is no doubt that our capacity to convey thoughts, ideas and feelings across space and time by preserving them on stone, parchment, paper and digitally has been transformational in the development of our species.

One of the most important skills parents can teach their children is to make them into readers from an early age. It will set them up for life. As teachers, we see the consequences when this doesn't happen, and trying to remedy a lack of reading ability later is possible but difficult. The non-reading child will always be at a disadvantage.

That's why we must take seriously our responsibility to teach reading explicitly with the pupils in our school. It can be too easy to assume that the primary school will have taught reading and that our job therefore is simply to 'do' reading – that is, to put texts in front of our pupils and then to set questions, in writing or orally, about the content, the ideas.

In reality, as literate adults we will be employing a range of higher-level reading skills. We will, for example:

- move quickly through and across texts;
- locate key bits of information;
- follow the broad gist of articles and accounts;
- question a writer's facts or interpretation;
- link one text with another;
- make judgements about whether one text is better than, more reliable than, or more interesting than another text.

These are the things, as teachers of most subjects, we will routinely do. They are also, in addition to basic comprehension skills, precisely the kinds of skills that our pupils need to develop. And, as we have seen throughout the book so far, unless we do this then essentially the word-rich get richer while the word-poor get poorer: that is, the pupils from the most linguistically supportive backgrounds will outpace the others and do better. This, I am contending, is not to do with intelligence or brightness: it is to do with having the language skills with which to interpret and express the world, and we should be making such skills available to the word-poor. They need us to do so.

This chapter therefore looks at reading in its widest sense. It gives ideas for helping our pupils to develop the range of skills they will need, chiefly by proposing that we make explicit the skills as adults we use implicitly. It looks also at ways we can make texts more accessible – how to frame questions, how to present handouts and worksheets – and how to help pupils with their spelling.

Teachers are often easily persuaded of the significant effect they can have in helping their pupils to write better; in my experience, we can have just as much impact, if perhaps less visible, when we explicitly teach reading skills.

There's one other aspect to reading too which is part of our responsibility: promoting the pleasure of reading. Many of us couldn't think of going on a journey or taking a holiday without taking books with us – whether electronic or old-fangled. The National Literacy Trust's depressing figures on reading habits (see page 12) show just how many young people don't have reading for pleasure or book ownership as part of their lives. It is, in many ways, a habit – a thing that we members of the Literacy Club routinely do.

This chapter therefore suggests ways in which we can promote the love of reading for the sake of reading, rather than as a functional activity. Again, it is a responsibility of all of us working in schools (not just teachers, and certainly not just English teachers) to show that reading stuff because we like reading stuff is one of the hallmarks of civilised adult life.

TALKING POINTS

- So what's your own reading history? How have your reading habits evolved and changed over the years?
- What kind of reading do you mostly do now?

What research tells us about reading

Reading matters a lot. It gives insights into the world, and into ourselves. But:

> . . . while good readers gain new skills very rapidly, and quickly move from *learning to read* to *reading to learn*, poor readers become increasingly frustrated with the act of reading, and try to avoid reading where possible.
>
> (Southwest Educational Development Laboratory, cited in Daniel Rigney, *The Matthew Effect*, p.76)

Reading isn't just decoding texts. Effective readers use a range of reading strategies. Siegler ('The Rebirth of Children's Learning', *Child Development 71:7*, 2000, cited in *Pedagogy and Practice: Unit 13 Developing Reading*, DfE, 2004) says that they acquire these by:

- observation (watching someone do it)
- discovery/invention (finding out for themselves)
- direct instruction (explain, show, tell, practise, feed back)
- analogy (if this works for X it might also work for Y).

'Students who begin with high verbal aptitudes find themselves in verbally enriched social environments and have a double advantage. Moreover, early success tends to create a virtuous cycle, in which the young reader learns to read faster, more, and with better comprehension, building on early advantage to achieve even larger advantages relative to peers' (Christine Nuttall, *Teaching Reading Skills in a Foreign Language*, Heinemann, 1996).

'Children who read slowly and without enjoyment read less' (Stanovitch, 'Matthew Effects in Reading: Individual Differences in the Acquisition of Literacy', *Reading Research Quarterly*, 1986).

'There may be a social dimension involved as well as good readers may choose friends who also read avidly while poor readers seek friends with whom they share other enjoyments' (Daniel Rigney, *The Matthew Effect*, p77).

'Researchers generally agree that early differences between good readers and poor readers tend to persist into adulthood and poor readers rarely catch up' (Daniel Rigney, *The Matthew Effect*, p.77).

Stricht's Law: 'reading ability in children cannot exceed their listening ability . . .' (cited in E.D. Hirsch, *The Schools We Need and Why We Don't Have Them*). This reinforces Hirsch's view that the best schools and teachers teach knowledge. He says: 'The children who possess intellectual capital when they first arrive at school have the mental scaffolding and Velcro to catch hold of what is going on, and they can turn the new knowledge into still more Velcro to gain still more knowledge' (p.20).

Implications

When it comes to reading, the stakes are very high. The link between being able to read independently and educational success are compelling. It's bleak to be reminded of how much this depends on parental and early years impact: the gap between the word-rich and word-poor begins to widen long before the pupils reach us in secondary schools.

That said, there's a salutary reminder here of our responsibility as teachers of any subject: we must not just 'do reading'; we must actively teach it – demonstrating and instructing pupils in the range of skills we take for granted.

Reading

This section of *Don't Call it Literacy!* explores various approaches and techniques which will help pupils in our classes to become better readers. Given the importance of being able to read well, there's a moral imperative on us all to become better at teaching our pupils to read better.

TALKING POINTS

● What are the main barriers your pupils face in reading in your subject – complicated vocabulary, long texts, a need for extensive prior knowledge?
● What do you already do to help pupils to read better?

How to evaluate the types of reading demands made in your subject

Different subjects will make different demands of pupils in terms of their reading. We will all, however, rely on reading as a skill – even if it is just at the level of reading from the whiteboard the instructions that we are giving our class.

A useful starting point for any teacher or subject team is therefore to begin to consider the range of reading skills we are expecting to use in our lessons and whether we are explicitly teaching these or simply leaving it up to pupils' own prior knowledge and experience – in which case we are abdicating responsibility for an essential skill.

Some starting points for reflecting upon reading:

1 Reading for information

● How do you read texts in your subject?

● What are the conventions of the texts (chronological? What type of linking words – next, then, as, whilst, however?).

● Do you model your reading with pupils, explaining how your interpret texts, how you cope with difficult words and concepts?

2 Teaching vocabulary and spelling

● What are the most significant words in your subject?

Reading

- Where can pupils see them, access them in your absence, and learn them?

- How do you help them to know how to spell them (see-hear-memorise)?

3 Using layout to make handouts more accessible

- We can help pupils to access texts by thinking how we set out worksheets and other resources. Are handouts clear and accessible?

- Are presentations uncluttered and in sensible colour combinations? Are key words listed at the beginning?

- Is the purpose of the text – why you are reading this/what you will learn – set out at the start?

- Are layout features used to make the text easier to access – short paragraphs, columns, bullet points, captions, key words, summaries?

4 Assessing reading

The default mode of assessment in the classroom is often questions following a text. These, as we shall see, can lead to the testing of superficial reading skills. Do you avoid a succession of narrow comprehension questions and instead use:

- Prediction: what do you think happens next?

- Cloze: which key words are missing?

- Disjunction: this text is in the wrong order – can you sort it out?

- Words to pictures: draw an illustration/graph to show what the text means at this point.

- Question variety: open-ended questions (Why? How?); true/false questions; question continuums (how far do you agree 1–5?); statements to agree with/argue against.

How to evaluate the types of reading in your subject

5 Promoting reading

- Do pupils see you reading, and talking about reading?
- Does your classroom showcase some of the great writers from your subject and what they have written – e.g. designers, scientists, chefs, philosophers?
- Do you read aloud texts so that pupils internalise the rhythms of English?
- Do you talk about texts you are reading for pleasure, irrespective of whether they are part of your subject or not?

TALKING POINTS

- What are the implications of this set of questions for you in your own teaching? What do you need to do more of and less of?
- What are the implications for the department as a whole or the school?

How to build a reading culture

It's easy for teachers – often the wizened cynics of the staffroom – to see the teaching of reading as someone else's job, such as the SENCO or the literacy coordinator. In reality, it's everyone's job. Every teacher in English is a teacher of English and nothing is more important than helping our pupils to develop a level of independence in their reading. It is a crucial life-skill.

Here's a set of questions for reflecting on personally or in a team meeting. They can be used to help drive a coherent whole-school approach to reading:

- When do pupils *see you reading*? Do they see you reading for pleasure or hear you talking about a text you're reading beyond your subject? Does your subject area have some of the great texts from your subject on display, exemplifying why reading matters?

- Do you read texts *aloud*, drawing attention to the way experts in your subject express ideas? Do you give time for pupils to read texts, in silence, followed by time to discuss and clarify what they have read?

- What are the *types of reading* pupils are expected to do in your subject (e.g. non-fiction reports, analyses, chronological accounts, poetry) and what reading skills (skimming, scanning, analyse, research) are they expected to know – how do you teach and model these?

- What are the main *barriers* to reading – sentence length, impersonal style, technical vocabulary?

- What are the *game-changing* words and phrases that help pupils to read, write and speak like an expert in your subject – e.g. 'analyse' or use of impersonal voice?

- What do you routinely do to help pupils to grasp and *practise* using these? Are these words on display in every classroom in your subject? Do you routinely use them, repeat them, and 'orally bracket' their meaning?

- What is the normal *reading level* of handouts and worksheets (using 'readability' statistics in Word under 'Grammar and Spelling')? Could you make texts more accessible by reducing sentence length, simplifying vocabulary, adding visual variety?

- How do you *frame* the texts you present to pupils: are they visually appealing, uncluttered, with a big question at the start, glossaries at the top, questions along the side, alternatives to questions (e.g. draw . . . cloze . . . re-order . . . predict . . . argue . . .)?

TALKING POINTS
- So as a teacher, department, school, which of these reading skills are you strongest and weakest at?
- What might you do as a result?

How to develop pupils' range of reading strategies

As we have seen, it is easy to take reading for granted. We can too easily dish out another set of textbooks or handouts, or put a PowerPoint on screen for pupils to absorb, without thinking of the reading strategies required to read, understand, interpret and respond.

Our starting point, therefore, is to think about the kind of reading skills confident readers use. The list on the facing page suggests some of the things that effective readers do. It's useful in, say, departmental meetings to start the process of looking at the texts you use and the skills you expect.

How to develop pupils' range of reading strategies

What effective readers do when they read:	*What this means:*
Predict	They make informed guesses about the text.
Skim	They read quickly through the sentences getting a gist of the understanding of the text.
Scan	Their eyes move across a text searching for a specific word/phrase/number.
Read closely	They pay close attention to the sentences, taking time to understand the meaning.
Question	They ask questions about a text to clarify your ideas.
Read backwards and forwards	They have the confidence to move through the text, including re-reading, to make connections or clarify ideas.
Empathise	They put themselves in someone else's shoes and feel what they feel.
Visualise	They see a picture in their minds to help gain a better impression or understanding of the text.
Infer	They read 'between the lines' to find the writer's intended meaning.

TALKING POINTS

- Which of these reading strategies is MOST and LEAST important in your subject?
- Which do you already teach explicitly? How?
- What might you do differently as a result of this chapter?

Reflecting on your own reading skills

Being fully paid-up members of the Literacy Club, we teachers often take for granted how well we ourselves read. It's worth reminding ourselves of just how adept we are in using language and in responding to texts.

Even the least confident teacher in the staffroom – who may be you – will have an extraordinarily well-developed ability to read and to make assumptions about unknown texts. If you don't believe me, this chapter is designed to demonstrate our literacy prowess. And if we can do this, what do we need to do to ensure that all pupils – including those from the most culturally disadvantaged backgrounds – can do the same?

Use the activity on your own or at a departmental meeting. Here are three short mystery texts. So for each one, say:

● What type of text is it (its genre or text-type)?

● Where would you find it (leaflet, poster, article, novel, etc)?

● How do you know?

Text A

Proud mum in a million Natalie Brown hugged her beautiful baby daughter Casey yesterday and said: 'She's my double miracle.'

Text B

The blood vessels of the circulatory system, branching into multitudes of very fine tubes (capillaries), supply all parts of the muscles and organs with blood, which carries oxygen and food necessary for life.

Text C

Ensure that the electrical supply is turned off. Ensure the existing circuit to which the fitting is to be connected has been installed and fused in accordance with current L.L.L. wiring regulations.

TALKING POINTS

- So what did you make of each text? How easy was it to say something about WHAT type of text it was?
- What were the main clues in each text that helped you to work out WHERE it might be found and HOW it is written?
- How successfully would your pupils do this task? What skills would they need to develop to become as adept as we are at responding to unseen texts?

LANGUAGE COMMENTARY

Text A is from the *Daily Mirror*. It uses alliteration, labels, and a tone of sentimentality that locates it as a tabloid newspaper story.

Text B is from a Biology textbook. The key feature is the way it uses a technical term ('circulatory system') and then uses more accessible language to clarify the meaning. It's what great teachers do too.

Text C is from a leaflet that accompanied an IKEA lamp we bought. It's an odd mixture – highly technical (implying it is written for electricians, say) and very basic (making the first sentence unnerving: we would like to think electricians already know this!).

How we skim texts

Skimming a text is reading to find the gist of it. Scanning a text is searching for specific information. These are skills we use a lot. Examine how we deploy them, bearing in mind that a lot of our literacy work as teachers is taking the skills we use implicitly and making them explicit.

Skimming

Read text A below. Give yourself 15 seconds to find out:

a) What is the text about?

b) Where would you find it?

c) How do you know?

As you do so, try to reflect on how you are reading.

> The climate of the Earth is always changing. In the past it has altered as a result of natural causes. Nowadays, however, the term climate change is generally used when referring to changes in our climate that have been identified since the early part of the 1900s. The changes we've seen over recent years and those that are predicted over the next 80 years are thought to be mainly as a result of human behaviour rather than due to natural changes in the atmosphere.

My guess is that when skimming the text, you realise that reading some words are more important than reading others: some words (lexical words such as 'climate, 'Earth' and 'changing') carry specific meanings while others (grammatical words such as 'the' and 'of') gum the lexical words together.

Confident readers, especially when under pressure of time, move their eyes over the lexical words in order to gain the main sense of the text's meaning. We make judgements about what the words refer to (their 'semantic fields') and whether the text seems impersonal and formal. Based on these judgements we narrow down the possibilities of what the text is.

Here is a demonstration of that skill. Look at what happens if you are presented with a text consisting only of grammatical words:

```
                        and           the

        of the              from the                    of
              . The            also    its    to the

      is          in the         with the        and in
           to                          but it            the
      that the
              his

      is the              in our        from the   , the
                    by              is     and a
 this          from the

 The             a        of                     that of the
                      in our              its    is
                        that of
```

What can you work out from this text? What is its topic? Is it fiction or non-fiction?

How are you reaching any judgements?

Reading

Then look what happens when one lexical word is added:

		and		the				
	of the		from the					of
		. The		also	its	to the		
is		in the		with the		and in		
	to				but it		the	
that the								
		his						
is the			in our		from the	, the		
			by		is	and a		
this		from the						
The		a	of				that of the	
				in our		its	is	
				that of Earth.				

Again, note what you do – what your brain does. Note how it latches onto the lexical word 'Earth' and the deduction it makes based on the capital 'E'.

This is what we do when we read – we make choices and decisions intuitively. Our job as teachers is to make the implicit judgements explicit – to demonstrate how reading works.

The box at the top of the facing page shows what the text looks like with all of its lexical words reinstated.

The capacity to skim a text – to get the gist of it – is an important skill that we can easily take for granted. In our lessons we could give pupils a sequence of 'mystery texts' – texts about our subject in different styles and genres – and present them as starter activities for pupils to guess their origin. This could be a game or competition.

The result of such activities is that pupils will become more confident in their reading, more familiar with a range of texts, and more aware of the various strategies the word-rich use to help gain a better understanding of a range of texts.

Facts and info about Planet Saturn

The name of the planet derives from the mythical Roman god Saturn, god of fertility, and agriculture. The god Saturn also gives its name to the word 'Saturday'.

Saturn is clearly visible in the night sky with the naked eye, and in consequence has been known to humans since prehistoric times, but it was not until the year 1659 that the astronomer Christian Huygens correctly identified Saturn's now famous rings using his telescope.

Saturn is the sixth furthest planet in our solar system from the sun, the average distance being 1427 million km; Earth by comparison is nine and a half times this distance away from the sun.

The planet Saturn has a diameter of about 120,536 km, eleven times that of the Earth, making it the second biggest planet in our solar system. Its mass is second only to Jupiter, and is 95 times greater than that of Earth.

TALKING POINTS

- How much do pupils in your subject need to be able to skim a text?
- What kinds of activities could you do to build their skills and confidence?

How we scan texts

Scanning

Scanning is when we search a text to find specific information. Here are three questions. Your task is to find the answers in the text that follows. As you do so, reflect on how you are approaching the task – what are the reading skills you are using?

The text below is about early mobile telephones. Answer the following:

- Where did the first cell phones begin?

- Name two other features that started to be included in phones.

- Why are cell phones especially useful in some countries?

Cellular telephones

The first cellular telephone system began operation in Tokyo in 1979, and the first U.S. system began operation in 1983 in Chicago. A camera phone is a cellular phone that also has picture-taking capabilities. Some camera phones have the capability to send these photos to another cellular phone or computer. Advances in digital technology and microelectronics has led to the inclusion of unrelated applications in cellular telephones, such as alarm clocks, calculators, Internet browsers, and voice memos for recording short verbal reminders, while at the same time making such telephones vulnerable to certain software viruses. In many countries with inadequate wire-based telephone networks, cellular telephone systems have provided a means of more quickly establishing a national telecommunications network.

So what are your answers to the three questions? How did you approach the task? My guess is that you once again deployed some of the intuitive knowledge that we have as teachers. We know that the answer to question two is more likely to be in the middle of the text, somewhere between the answers to questions one and three. It's another indication of how we can easily take for granted the conventions of reading, rather than making them explicit to the pupils we teach.

TALKING POINTS
- How much scanning of texts do pupils need to do in your subject?
- How do you teach them the skills required? How could you use a sequence of starter activities or games that would build their confidence in locating specific information?

How to encourage pupils to read texts actively

It can be too easy to give pupils a text followed by a list of questions. While we may feel that these are helping to develop pupils' reading skills, they can in fact be entirely superficial.

The best-known demonstration of this is 'Glombots'. Read the text and then answer the questions:

> Glombots, who looked durly and lurkish, were very fond of wooning, which they usually did in the grebble rather than the grimper.

- What did Glombots look like?
- What were they fond of doing?
- Where did they go wooning?
- Why do you think they preferred the grebble to the grimper for wooning?

You should find it fairly straightforward to get 100% for these questions – without understanding at all what Glombots are.

It's a sign of the way traditional comprehension questions could reinforce a superficial surface approach to reading.

DARTs – directed activities related to texts – were a fashionable alternative approach to traditional comprehension questions in the 1980s and 1990s, which are now swinging back into vogue. They require pupils to interact with texts in a way that takes them beneath the surface. These activities are most effective when worked on by a pair or small group as the discussion of possibilities leads to a closer look at the text. They consist of the following:

Cloze

Give pupils a text with some key words missing. Skills include:

- paying close attention to the meaning of the sentence;
- choosing a word that fits grammatically;
- using one's existing knowledge of the topic;
- working out what is likely from the rest of the text;
- working out what will fit with the style of the text;
- working out whether a word has already occurred in the sentence;
- attending to the sense of the whole sentence by reading and rereading.

Sequencing

Give pupils a text that has been cut into chunks. Skills include:

- reading and rereading;
- paying close attention to the structure of the genre;
- paying close attention to link words;
- hunting for the logic or organising principle of the text – e.g. chronological order;
- using previous experience and earlier reading.

Reading

Text marking

Get pupils reading a text actively. Text marking includes under-lining, annotating or numbering the text to show sequence. Skills may well include:

- skimming or scanning to find specific information;
- differentiating between different categories of information;
- deciding what is relevant information;
- finding the main idea(s);
- questioning the information presented in the text.

Text restructuring

Get pupils to interpret a text in a different form. Text restructuring involves reading and then remodelling the information in another format. For example, flow charts, diagrams, Venn diagrams, grids, lists, maps, charts, concept maps or rewriting in another genre. Depending on the format, skills used will include:

- identifying what is key and relevant in a text;
- applying what they know in a new context;
- remodelling the content and the format of the text;
- awareness of the characteristics of different genres;
- critical reading;
- summary and prioritisation;
- writing as well as reading skills.

TALKING POINTS
- Which of these reading approaches do you currently use?
- What kinds of texts and activities would they help pupils to make progress in your subject?

How to develop pupils' analytical skills in reading

In general, as we get better at reading we move from 'what' (a basic level of comprehension) to 'who' (being able to comment on who wrote a text and who it is aimed at) to the higher level skills, which involve analysis and evaluation: the 'how' of a text.

Having a common understanding of this across subjects can be really useful for pupils, as well as giving them a framework for knowing what kinds of clues to look for when evaluating a writer's attitude or style.

Here is a simple approach to moving pupils from the 'what' to the 'how' in their reading, and provides a framework for them to look for when commenting on language.

WHAT:

● What is the text about?

● What type of text is it (informative, persuasive, entertaining)?

WHO:

● Who wrote it?

● Who is it written for (general audience, specialist, younger/ older)?

Reading

HOW:

Structure:

- Chronological (a story) or non-chronological (a report)? Why?
- Short/long paragraphs? Why?
- How are ideas linked (connectives such as 'first'; pronouns such as 'he')?

Sentences:

- Statements, questions, commands? Why?
- Short or long? Why?
- Formal or colloquial?

Words:

- Formal ('is not') or informal ('isn't')?
- Personal ('I'/'you') or impersonal ('it')?
- Serious or humorous?
- General ('ill') or specialist ('supra-renal')?
- Accessible ('clumsy') or inaccessible ('maladroit')?

TALKING POINTS

- This framework was developed for work in English. Which parts of it apply in your subject?
- What are the 'structure, sentence and word' level barriers to learning for pupils you teach: which elements do they find hardest?

How to help pupils to spell more accurately

Spelling in English is a bit like algebra in Maths: it's rooted in our concept of identity, of self-esteem. If we perceive ourselves as bad spellers or bad at Maths, then we can too easily assume we are not very bright.

In reality, even the best of us at spelling will have words that we struggle with, and strategies that we apply to help us to spell those words accurately.

It gives huge support to these pupils, if as teachers we take a common approach to spelling:

- Break it into sounds *(u-n-i-o-n)*
- Break it into syllables *(con-tin-ent)*
- Break it into affixes *(dis + satisfy)*
- Use a mnemonic *(Never Eat Chips Eat Salad Sandwiches And Remain Young!)*
- Refer to a word in the same family *(chemical, chemist, chemistry)*
- Over-articulate it *(Wed-nes-day)*
- Words within words *(GUM in argument)*
- Refer to word history *(bi = two, cycle = wheels)*
- Use analogy *(through, rough, enough)*

Reading

● Use a key word *(I'm – to remember an apostrophe can replace a missing letter)*

● Apply spelling rules *(hopping = short vowel sound, hoping = long vowel)*

The most important thing we can do as a teacher is to show pupils that we all have spelling blind-spots – words we struggle to spell accurately. They need to hear from us the techniques we use to help us to spell correctly. Simply modelling that – saying, for example, 'when I write "government" I say it in my head as "govern–ment": I emphasise the "n" in the middle' – helps to demystify spelling for our students.

This is what we do in the Literacy Club: we have our own literacy strategies. We should share them with our pupils.

TALKING POINTS

● On page 164 there are lists of words from different subjects. How might you use these to help pupils to spell them more accurately in your subject?

● Where do pupils currently encounter these words – are they on display in your subject area?

How to help pupils to revise

Revision for exams can be the most deadly part of our teaching repertoire, especially if it consists of a succession of past papers. Revision ought to be some of our more creative teaching, given that our pupils will know most of the content.

Here, then, are sixty-eight ideas for 'revving up revision':

Starting points:

1   We should try to see things from the pupil's point of view: they haven't sat major exams before, they don't know what to expect, and they will appreciate clear, practical, unpatronising advice.

2   If we don't teach pupils how to revise, then it's an equal opportunities issue: those from supportive backgrounds will do better than those who have to fend for themselves.

3   Good revision won't be a succession of past papers. It will be a process within lessons and across the final stage of a course that moves pupils from dependence to independence.

4   In good revision the teacher will do increasingly less while the pupils do increasingly more.

5   We should teach knowledge and skills and techniques, but recognise that the best teachers may be other pupils, and possibly slightly older ones.

6   Literacy skills are crucial in most exams – the terminology that distinguishes middle from top grades, the skills needed for reading papers and organising answers, and – most significantly – writing skills.

7   The most powerful way we will help our pupils to do better in exams is therefore possibly by doing shared writing (composition – planning – demonstration).

8   Students – especially boys – improve their writing skills when allowed very brief spoken opportunities to discuss what they will write.

9   We should be realistic telling pupils that most revision sessions should last no more than 25 minutes, followed by a built-in reward. Let's give them realistic revision skills that fit into their lifestyle. Teach the Pomodoro Technique.

Teaching what revision looks like:

10 Get some sixth form pupils who did your subject last year to come and do speed dating with groups of pupils – how they revised, which bits they found easiest/hardest, which revision approaches worked best: all of this humanises the process of revision.

11 Get pupils to devise a chart, map, plan or grid, which shows the key bits of knowledge and the key skills they will need to develop. In any revision session get them to map where it fits with the big picture.

12 Get pupils to create a timeline of what they will know by when and how they should be able to demonstrate it.

13 Have a downloadable summary of key skills and knowledge posted on the homework forum.

14 Use a traffic lights system for pupils to colour bits they feel very confident about (green), less so (yellow) and weak on (red).

15 Use the traffic lights for pupils to talk to a sixth form pupil who took your subject last year about bits they can and can't do.

16 Teach pupils how to make summaries, to synthesise key points, to make spider diagrams, to create mind maps: demonstrate how to do these.

17 Feed information about pupils' revision skills (e.g. how much MyMaths they have been doing) to their active mentor, so that progress is noted and praised.

Reinforcing learning:

18 Explain this concept to me as if I'm a 6-year old or grandparent.

19 Explain this concept in a spider diagram.

20 Explain this concept in a sequence of three pictures – no words allowed.

21 Create a poster of six words that sum up all the key information in this topic. Then explain your words to a partner.

22 Play a true/false quiz with key concepts.

23 Display key words around the classroom and occasionally test pupils on their meaning.

24 Give an extract of a text with key words missing: ask pupils to work out what the concepts are.

25 Get some sixth form pupils to put together a comprehensive list of websites that are useful for revision. Put this on the Homework Forum.

26 Teach memory skills by doing a series of starter activities in which pupils have to learn facts or concepts quickly and under pressure. Get some pupils to explain to others how they approached the task and managed to learn things.

27 Teach pupils how we can memorise through visualising (e.g. create a journey of the things you have to remember) or sound (make up silly mnemonics/jingles).

28 Set up speed dating to test each other/answer questions/ demonstrate how much they know on a topic.

Applying knowledge:

29 Ask students to write the first part of a model answer (the first paragraph will do), then share it with a partner to get feedback on how clear, accurate and knowledgeable it is – i.e. focus on small sections at first.

30 In groups, ask pupils to design and write one page of a revision textbook. You collate them into one document and publish it on the Homework Forum – a tailor-made revision guide.

31 Every lesson, as a starter, brainstorm the key concepts pupils need, asking them to explain/define/summarise key ideas.

32 Ask pupils in small groups to think up a question, to produce the answer, and to write the guidance a chief examiner would provide. Look at sample questions to help get the tone and style right.

33 Take an exam question and annotate it – showing what the key words are that pupils must know; better still, get pupils to do this.

34 Take an exam answer or three and annotate them, showing what pupils need to know about the difference between a C, B and A*.

35 Play *Mastermind* to reinforce knowledge.

36 Play *Who Wants to Be a Millionaire* with pupils posing the questions, knowing the answers, and structuring them from easy to hard.

37 Play 'Splat!' where pupils have to run to the part of the room displaying the right answer to a question you read aloud.

38 Play word associations, saying some key words and asking pupils to see what comes into their head. This will tell you how embedded their revision is.

39 Produce a revision podcast for other groups.

40 Design a leaflet for Year 10 that summarises key concepts.

41 Produce a rap to help pupils memorise the key concepts of your course.

42 Roll a dice and ask questions relating to one subject – pupils have 10 seconds to think about what they will say before (no hands up) answering.

43 Write a 'bad' first paragraph to a question. Ask students to annotate it to show why it's not great.

44 Play starter activities that help pupils to know the key connectives of their subject – *although, as, because, despite, however*, and so on.

45 Display the key spellings that pupils will need.

46 Design a courtroom exercise in which one pupil or more answers other pupils' questions on key topics.

47 Look at past exam or sample questions and answers and let pupils annotate the key features.

48 We only truly know something when we can teach it to others. Group pupils with others in different groups or years. Their challenge is to teach the other/younger pupils the skills they have learnt, and then to get feedback on how clear and accessible they made the subject.

Focus on reading skills:

49 Teach the reading skills pupils will need in your subject, both for revision and for the exam – e.g. skimming, scanning, analysing.

50 Take past questions and put them into a PowerPoint, one question per slide. Get pupils thinking of the key words and phrases they should be looking for; then flash the slides up, getting pupils to tell you the important information in each question. This applies to Maths as much as any other subject.

Reading

51 If pupils have to read lots of text in an exam, practise the skill through a sequence of starters, which flash different texts in front of them. Give them a small amount of time and, working in pairs or groups, get them to skim a text (get the gist) or scan a text (find specific information). This will build confidence in their reading.

52 Show them how in an exam you might read actively – highlighting or underlining key words.

Focus on writing skills:

53 Take an exam question and get pupils to think of the opening sentence of a BAD answer. Then ask them to explain why it's bad (bad answers help to build confidence and to focus on the essential skills for success).

54 Model a good answer on the board, listening to pupils' comments and advice. Students need to see that when we write, all of us make errors, think and correct ourselves frequently.

55 Make sure pupils know the conventions of writing in your subject (should they use the passive voice in Science ['potassium was added to the test tube' rather than 'I added potassium to the test tube']?, should they avoid using 'I' and 'me' in analytical work in History and Technology; should they use an introduction that says 'in this essay I am going to show . . .' or just dive into the answer?).

56 If pupils are expected to provide evidence to support their points (e.g. quotations in English Lit), demonstrate how to bed these into existing sentences.

57 Demonstrate how good writing uses connectives, which help to guide a reader through a text – e.g. 'First . . . Later . . . Another way of looking at this . . . In conclusion'.

58 Teach pupils how to take notes, showing them that we all have a preferred style (e.g. spider diagrams, bullet points, mind maps, etc).

59 Give them practice in making notes – dictate a boring lecture on something obscure; do it at a fast pace. Their job is to make notes that will allow them to answer ten questions on what they have heard.

60 Put some sample revision cards/notes on display to help pupils know what they might look like.

61 Ask some sixth form pupils to explain and demonstrate the form of note-making they used.

Guide pupils on creating the conditions for learning:

62 Talk with pupils about where they work, how they work, how they cope with distractions, how they resist laziness, how they reward themselves, whether they use music in the background; get some older pupils to talk about this.

63 Talk to pupils about how examiners work, who they are, what they look for and how to make a good impression from the first page of the answer book.

64 Ask pupils to show you their traffic lighted revision plan.

65 Put together a mini revision guide for parents – questions they could ask, ways they could help their child.

66 Praise pupils who attend revision sessions and booster classes.

67 Write a note or card to each pupil, wishing them well.

68 Remind pupils of how they can get support and guidance once study leave begins.

TALKING POINTS

● How do revision skills currently get taught in your subject?
● Which ideas here could bring a new approach?

How to help pupils to develop independent study skills

It can be too easy for secondary teachers to assume that the teaching of reading is the role of primary school teachers. In reality, we are all learning to read all the time and the explicit teaching of the skills we take for granted, even as accomplished readers, should characterise all lessons.

Here's an outline of the stages we might envisage for the secondary students we teach:

The emerging reader

Students start to move from 'learning to read' to 'reading to learn':

- The teacher models *how to read* certain types of texts and questions – e.g. how to analyse, how to spot main themes, how to untangle and make sense of complicated expression.

- We explicitly teach *key vocabulary* – subject-specific terms and the essential connectives of our subject (e.g. 'therefore', 'however', 'similarly').

- Students are given *additional reading* to work on semi-independently so that they practise what they have learnt.

The dependent reader

Students develop greater confidence in reading, but are still guided by the teacher:

● Students routinely read a range of *increasingly demanding* texts and respond to questions and tasks.

● Students routinely use the *key vocabulary* of the subject.

● Students' *wider reading* is prescribed and monitored.

The independent reader

Students develop greater self-direction, routinely employing a range of reading strategies to deepen their understanding:

● Students routinely read analytically, and can cite the *key thinkers/ideas* in their subject.

● Students routinely use the *key vocabulary* of their subject – in speech and writing.

● Students show a *reflective ability* to question the 'how' and 'why' of sources and ideas – an ability to make judgements about what they read.

TALKING POINTS
● So what progress in reading do the pupils you teach make? How do you know?
● How could you more systematically promote and monitor their reading progress?

How to promote independent research

Imagine you are a Year 9 pupil, and your History teacher has set you homework on researching Martin Luther King. What do you do?

In the past you would have headed to the library, in school or near home, and grabbed a copy of Encyclopaedia Britannica. But now you're more likely to reach for Google. And that's where we suddenly see that the landscape of independent research has changed. Because now there isn't a reliable trusted source from which you can immediately gain knowledge. Google is a gateway rather than a source of information.

And if we look at martinlutherking.org we get many of the signs that this is a site we can rely on. There's the authoritative url; the fact that the site describes itself as providing a 'true historical examination'. In fact, the site is one run by white supremacists.

So when we talk about encouraging pupils' independent research skills we need to be careful that we're not abdicating all responsibility and leaving youngsters to navigate a potentially dark and troubled route into cyberspace.

Every department that requires research needs to teach research. As teachers we need to model the choices we make, the decisions we encounter, the links we follow and those we reject; we need to show how – as members of the Literacy Club – we decide what is trustworthy on the internet and what is not. We need to take our implicit assumptions and make them explicit. Otherwise we're failing in our duty to pass on important literacy skills to the next generation and consigning them to encountering websites that are at best dodgy and at worst downright harmful.

TALKING POINTS

- So what independent research do you expect of pupils in your subject? How do you help pupils to learn the necessary skills?
- What opportunities are there for developing pupils' skills across different subjects? And what role could your school library and librarian play in this?

How do we promote 'reading for pleasure'?

My father was a librarian. That had a big influence. Like lots of people, I couldn't imagine surviving without books. Because I like the feel of books and the smell of books, I haven't wholeheartedly embraced the e-book phenomenon. As a result I have to smuggle books into our house and add them discreetly to our groaning bookcases. Yes: I like books.

And the thing is I can't imagine what it must be like for our pupils not to like books too. That's why I couldn't conceive of a library stripped of its books and reconfigured as a 'learning resource centre'. Our pupils need to encounter books, to see their ongoing relevance, and to see the way they have shaped our culture.

Ofsted don't have a thing to say about reading for pleasure. That doesn't mean they don't think it's important. Rather, it's that they haven't written much about it – perhaps, shamefully, because they haven't seen much evidence of it in our schools.

Ofsted's latest guidance on promoting reading says this:

> *English at the crossroads*, which summarised findings from inspections of English between 2005 and 2008, suggested that although schools, especially primary schools, devoted a considerable amount of time to reading, few had a coherent and consistently articulated policy on developing reading skills. They used a range of strategies but, often, in a fragmented way.

For example, 'guided reading' (targeted reading activities in small groups, often adult-led) was often taught as a discrete activity and not linked to reading in English lessons. If anything, provision to encourage independent reading in secondary schools was even less developed.

Excellence in English highlighted case studies from successful schools where promoting reading is a high priority. The report identified a curriculum that gives high priority to reading for pleasure as one of the key components in producing excellence.

One of the key aspects of effective reading in primary schools, as shown in these case studies, is the determination of staff to promote a culture that encourages pupils to enjoy reading, share their views on what they have read and develop the ability to compare texts and express opinions about them.

Bleakly, they have little to say about reading for pleasure in secondary schools. It's as if it's disappeared as an issue. Not for me it hasn't. So here are some thoughts on promoting reading for pleasure:

- Reject the idea of silent reading in tutor time. It appeals to some headteachers as a superficial demonstration of reading for pleasure. In reality it's usually nothing of the sort. My son Nick went to a school that had 'reading lessons'. When I asked him what they were like he said 'Well, actually they're "let's pretend we're reading" lessons'. There was always half the class without a book, the teacher too stressed by a backlog of marking, an environment that was hardly conducive to losing yourself in a good book. So let's – please – eschew reading lessons.

- Instead let's explore the idea of 'reading communities'. This, trendy as it sounds, is what we readers do – we talk about books. Let's group pupils around a particular text – a story, a poem, an article, and then give them some open questions (how and why) that encourage them to discuss what they have read. It's fine for them to read in silence, but it's for a purpose, and doesn't associate reading with authoritarian, passive, soulless control.

119

Reading

- Make the library the vibrant hub of the school. Locate all the good stuff there – talks, debating society, parents' evenings, talks by visiting writers. Make it feel like a place you can't resist visiting.

- Make reading central to the school culture. Get in writers. Link your newsletter with a local bookshop so that taking the newsletter to the shop results in a discount. Incentivise reading – pupils who attend talks miss lessons to be there (sorry!). Use images to celebrate reading.

- Talk about reading. Sod what's in the lesson plan: if you've read an interesting story, extract, article or biography, or anything, take it in and read it. More than ever, we need to show our pupils that reading matters. That means reading stuff aloud, laughing at it, getting upset at it, and celebrating it. It may prove a more important element in your lesson than you will ever realise.

TALKING POINTS

- So what do you do in your classroom, department and school to promote reading for pleasure?
- What could you do next?

LANGUAGE COMMENTARY

The first paragraph of this chapter illustrates the way I write and the way I teach my pupils to write. It contains a mix of short sentences and long sentences, of formal vocabulary ('phenomenon') with informal vocabulary ('big'), and it tries to be visual or unexpected – as in the image of the 'groaning bookshelves' (which probably isn't very original, but may help the reader to visualise the scene). I just thought I'd describe what I think I'm doing as I write.

PART FOUR

Writing

Introduction

Writing has been one of the weakest areas of teaching. The assumption too often is that imparting knowledge – making sure our pupils know stuff – is enough. In reality, of course the main way that most knowledge is assessed, whether in exams or controlled assessment or coursework, is through pupils' writing. It's something that needs to be taught.

Take these two examples: 'In the book the writer says' and 'In the novel the author suggests'. The vocabulary in sentence two is more precise and would earn a higher grade. But I'm not convinced it's a sign of greater intelligence. It may be that the pupil writing it has a teacher who explicitly teaches the discourse of his subject.

Or take these examples: 'At the start of the play Macbeth is a hero, but at the end he is a villain', compared with 'Although he starts the play a hero, Macbeth ends it a villain'. This time the difference isn't just vocabulary, it's also sentence structure. That connective 'although' enables the pupil to express an idea with greater complexity and elegance. It may be that he's a product of a bookish background, or of a teacher who has taught him how to do it.

Writing, in other words, matters a lot. It's how we express ourselves, how we give our opinions, our theories, our connecting

Writing

points with other humans. It's too important for us not to teach explicitly. And, as always, we're not asking teachers here to do anything technical or beyond their zone of direct experience: we're asking them merely to help their pupils to write like a designer or artist or musician or scientist. It is, in other words, about teaching and learning, our core business.

One other thing: in this section we look also at teacher writing – the kinds of writing teachers need to undertake for parents and colleagues. Too many of us feel a bit insecure when faced with the pedants of the staffroom, so part of this section is designed to build your own confidence in writing.

TALKING POINTS

- What kind of writing do pupils have to do in your subject? How do you help them?
- How confident are you in your own writing? Are there words you avoid because of spelling, or aspects of punctuation that you are insecure about? What do you do as a result?

What research tells us about writing

Many of us believe that pupils do too much writing in school. That means – wait for it – too much meaningless writing. One of the early gurus on this topic was James Britton who in 1975 taught us that boys in particular benefit from 'authentic' writing tasks.

This has clearly taken some time to bed in as Ofsted's 2009 report *English at the Crossroads* lamented the absence of 'real' tasks. Thus in English pupils would be asked to 'write a letter to a friend describing your summer holidays'. This, when we think about it, beggars belief. Which child nowadays would (a) write a letter to a friend and (b) write to them about such a topic?

According to Hillocks, the key ingredients in writing therefore appear to involve the teacher using three broad approaches:

● Presentational – setting tasks and marking outcomes.

● Process – where the pupils have some choice of tasks and writing is developed through drafts and 'peer conferencing'.

● Environmental – an ugly word describing something we now take for granted – the teacher using strategies and genres to help pupils to write better.

Writing is best when it arises from reading. That doesn't, however, mean just displaying a good model of a text on the interactive whiteboard. Teaching writing is more active than that. It involves:

Writing

- Modelling (the teacher sharing information about a text).

- Joint construction (teacher and pupils working together to create a text in the spirit of collaboration).

- Independent construction – when appropriate, pupils constructing a text in a new genre, still with the oversight of peers and the teacher.

To quote Myhill and Fisher (2010): 'Spoken language forms a constraint, a ceiling not only on the ability to comprehend but also on the ability to write, beyond which literacy cannot progress.' This, for me, is one of the most significant bits of research. We need to improve pupils' use of spoken English if we are to improve their written English. The pupil who tells a teaching assistant to 'F off' will perhaps not realise that disagreement can be expressed in a variety of ways, including in sentences that do not contain two words, one of which is 'off'.

The active teaching of vocabulary and sentence structures appears to make a big difference to pupils' ability to write well. In particular the teacher's role in modelling writing (which is more than just demonstrating it) seems to help pupils to see that writing is a process rather than a pre-packaged product.

TALKING POINTS

- Any surprises here? What are the implications for your own classroom?
- What do you currently do that helps the pupils you teach to become better writers?

Five things every teacher ought to know about writing

1   Remember *The Matthew Effect*: 'The rich will get richer and the poor will get poorer.' Unless we deliberately teach the writing skills pupils need in our subject, we will increase existing inequalities.

2   *Presentation matters.* The pupils who forget to bring rulers to school are the ones who most need them. We must be more insistent on work being properly set out, dates and titles underlined, margins left, etc. It's now an Ofsted priority, but perhaps we should have been more insistent about levels of presentation anyway.

3   *Demonstrating writing matters.* We need to show pupils how to write like a historian/scientist/musician/designer. This means modelling and demonstrating writing. It means making mistakes, correcting them, explaining your thought processes. At heart it's about making implicit processes explicit. It also must involve talking.

4   *Structure matters.* (a) To get a C or higher in any subject, pupils will need to be able to use paragraphs (rule-of-thumb three to five paragraphs to a page). (b) Students tend to link ideas in long sentences using 'and' and 'so'. Therefore teach them to write in *short and long sentences*. Short sentences at the start and ends of paragraphs give clarity and authority. (c) Teach

Writing

useful *connectives* to link ideas, such 'as', 'when', 'although', 'because' and 'despite'.

5 *Vocabulary matters*. The precision of the words we use marks the difference between the amateur and the expert. Teach key vocabulary by repeating words with definitions four times in a lesson. Technical terms build confidence. Don't shy away from teaching complex words to pupils you may consider less able: they may be the ones who benefit most.

TALKING POINTS

● Which of these points is familiar and which is unfamiliar?
● What do you recall about how you learnt to write – both the mechanics and improving your style?
● Who or what has had the most positive effect on your writing?

How to write: seven hints

Despite having a degree in their chosen subject, many teachers lack confidence in writing; and many members of school management teams can be heard lamenting the quality of written reports by staff.

This topic might therefore seem an unexpected one, a patronising inclusion, but it's here because for staff and pupils there are a small number of rules which make our writing clearer, more precise and more interesting.

1   Keep it brief. In writing that is poor, sentences are often too long and unwieldy. Keep the texts that you write brief and accessible: aim for one side of A4. If you must write more, provide a summary box of key points.

2   See everything from your readers' viewpoint: what will help them to absorb your ideas as efficiently as possible? It may be that certain layout features would help them – e.g. bold, boxes, bullet points, spacing, sub-headings.

3   Don't overload your sentences with ideas. Several short sentences will do the job better than an over-long one. For example, a text of two sentences:

> Seven of the 33 buildings in St James's Square, in the heart of one of the most expensive parts of the West End, display For Sale or To Let signs. The sight of some of the capital's

most exclusive business addresses languishing empty – when not long ago they were snapped up as corporate headquarters – brings home the impact of the recession as financial controllers cut costs by letting out spare space vacated by staff who have been made redundant or exiled to less costly locations.

A text of five sentences:

St James's Square is in the heart of one of the most expensive parts of the West End. Seven of the 33 buildings display For Sale or To Let signs. Some of the capital's most exclusive business addresses languish empty, when not long ago they were snapped up as corporate headquarters. This brings home the impact of the recession. Financial controllers have cut costs by letting out spare space vacated by staff who have been made redundant or exiled to less costly locations.

4 Use short sentences at the start and end of paragraphs: they give clarity to our topic, helping our readers to know what the main topic of the paragraph is and what our opinion or point is:

Another concern is cost. Although there are many external factors that can affect costs, we do have some control. We should be putting pressure on our suppliers to show greater market awareness, and to engage in a realistic dialogue with us about fair prices. At the moment there is often confusion about costs. **It is important to change this**.

5 Be clear about punctuation:

- *Full stops* to signal the end of a sentence.
- *Commas* to separate items in a list or create islands of words ('The decision, which had been made much earlier in the day, proved an important one').
- Dashes* – in pairs – to create emphasis ('It was a decision – though no one knew this at the time – that would change history').

- *Colons*: signal something to follow.
- *Semi-colons* allow us either to link related ideas or emphasise contrasts: 'The decision was significant; it would always be remembered' and 'summer brought pain; winter brought relief'.

6   Avoid clichés (ready-made phrases)

- A hands-on approach (practical)
- The jury is still out (is not yet decided)
- Meet with (meet)
- Put in place (prepare)
- Take on board (accept)
- User-friendly (easy to use)

7   Avoid unnecessary repetition (tautology):

- Absolute certainty (certainty)
- Added bonus (bonus)
- Added extra (extra)
- Quite distinct (distinct)
- End result (result)
- Past history (history)
- Really excellent (excellent)
- Revert back (return)

TALKING POINTS

- Writing in a variety of short and then longer sentences is probably the most useful advice we can give our pupils: is it a technique you use?
- How would you characterise your attitude to writing and your level of self-confidence?
- What advice in this section resonates with you and which do you disagree with?

LANGUAGE COMMENTARY

*I'm a bit of a fan of using punctuation parenthetically – that is, in pairs, like brackets (the Greek words for brackets is parentheses). The result, I suspect, is that I may overuse them. I like the clarity they can bring, the subtlety and – even with dashes – the ability to move key ideas into the background or foreground. You see: the bit between the paired commas and brackets is given a different kind of weight? And, yes, I teach every class of every age about parenthetical commas and dashes. Most pupils, it must be said, quietly humour me by nodding as if interested.

How to improve the accuracy of your own writing

Every staffroom has its pedants – those who tut-tut at the woeful standards of written English used by (tick as appropriate) teachers/ teaching assistants/admin staff/students/the headteacher.

We have to remember that we have a generation or two of teachers who were not taught by prescriptivist English teachers (those who, like the teacher I've become, are strong on rules of usage). It means they can often feel uncertain.

So, for a number of sources, I've compiled a usage guide for teachers. It's especially designed for quick reference before writing reports.

Some readers will hate it and find it pompous or patronising or insulting. Me: I love a bit of clarity, and since this is my book I'm including it.

- Affect/effect – affect is a verb relating to emotion or pretentiousness/affectation ('The man affects an American accent'; 'he was genuinely affected by the music'); effect is usually a noun ('His arrival had a big effect') but can be used as a verb meaning to change ('She effected changes as soon as she was appointed')

- A lot, not alot

- All sorts, not alsorts

Writing

- Basically: this word is unnecessary in most contexts
- Continuous/continual – a continuous noise never stops; a continual noise is frequent but with interruptions
- Comprise or consists of (but not 'comprises of')
- Dependant/dependent: a dependant is a noun ('he looked after his dependants'); dependent is an adjective ('they were dependent upon him')
- Different from, not different than
- Discreet – modest/restrained; discrete – separate
- Disinterested – neutral/objective; uninterested – not interested
- Due to – because of
- Every day: noun and adverb ('it happens every day'); everyday: adjective ('an everyday remark')
- Formally – being formal; formerly – in the past
- Fraction: use with care – saying 'he only produced a fraction of the necessary work' isn't the same as saying 'a small fraction' since 9/10 is a fraction
- Homogeneous – of the same kind; homogenous – of common descent
- Imply/infer – I imply that you are mad; you infer that I am being rude
- It's (it is/it has); its (the cat licked its paws)
- Like: use 'as if' – it looks as if he will be late
- Led – past tense of to lead; lead – rope for a dog and heavy element
- Less/fewer – less for quantities (I'll have less water); fewer than for items that can be individually counted (fewer than 10 bottles)
- Literally: use with care – not 'He literally jumped out of his skin'

132

How to improve the accuracy of your own writing

- Meet – not meet with
- Momentarily – he stopped momentarily, not the Americanism I'll be there momentarily
- More than – better than over (it cost more than £27)
- No one, not no-one
- Onto – doesn't exist. The phrase is on to
- Prevaricate – to lie or deceive; procrastinate – to put something off
- Principal – head of a school; principle/principles – beliefs
- Program – runs on a computer; programme – something we watch on television or buy at a theatre
- Theirs (no apostrophe)
- Try to, not try and
- Under way, not underway
- Until, not up until
- Upcoming: avoid
- While, not whilst
- Yours (no apostrophe)
- Outside, not outside of

TALKING POINTS
- Helpful or patronising?
- What points of usage in this guide are new to you?
- Would something similar be useful for pupils?

Evaluating the main writing ingredients needed for your subject

Every subject will have different conventions and expectations for the dominant types of writing. An evaluation in Design Technology, for example, probably shouldn't begin like this: 'I really enjoyed making this CD holder . . .' It demands a style that is more impersonal, more formal, more detached.

The set of questions shown on the facing page is designed to help you to identify the key writing ingredients needed in writing in your subject.

TALKING POINTS

- Which of these points is the easiest to teach and which do pupils struggle most with?
- What is the best advice you were given about writing in your subject?

Evaluating writing ingredients for your subject

Convention	Relevant questions
Layout	Are there any conventions about layout – e.g. use of paragraphs, bullet points, headlines, sub-headings, bold, italic, quotations? Do pupils know them?
Structure	Is the text chronological (telling a story from start to finish)? If not, how should it be structured? Do the big ideas come first, or the arguments for and then the arguments against? Is an introduction needed? A conclusion? How should these sound?
Formality	How formal should the text be: should pupils use 'isn't' and 'don't'? Should they use abbreviations like 'etc'? Should they use technical words? Are polysyllabic words generally better than monosyllabic words ('suggest' rather than 'say', 'disappointing' rather than 'bad')?
Impersonality	Should pupils avoid using 'I'? Should they use the passive voice ('Potassium was added to the test-tube' rather than 'I added potassium to the test-tube')? Should a personal opinion be included at the end? Is the pronoun 'we' generally more advisable than using 'I'?
Vocabulary	What kind of words should pupils use? Which are the ones used by the experts in your subject? How do pupils know these? Where do they see them? How do they access them if you are off sick? Can you help pupils to spell key words accurately (visual/auditory/mnemonics)?

How to teach pupils to write

We don't teach writing by showing pupils model texts, even if we annotate them to show their good features. We teach writing by writing.

In an age of ready-made online resources and interactive whiteboards, we can give our pupils a mistaken impression that writing is a product rather than a process. They need to see that writing is something involving decisions and mistakes. They need to see us – their teachers in all subjects – writing stuff.

As a sequence this will involve:

- Thinking about the 'what' and the 'how' of a text – what its *purpose* is and who its *audience* is. Those considerations will affect how we write it (how it is set out, how formal it is, and so on).

- We will want to explore some of the *conventions* of the text – whether to do with layout (short paragraphs, bullet points) or language (impersonal style).

- Next, and most importantly, we will want to *demonstrate* how we might write the text. That means pupils watching as we articulate the decisions we need to make and invite them to comment. It will sound something like this:

> I want to write this as a scientist. That means it's the process of the experiment that's important, not the person

who did it. So my first sentence will describe what happened without mentioning 'I' or 'me' at all. Think about what your opening sentence might be and say it to a partner – no need to write it down. Then let's hear some of your examples and compare them with what I am thinking.

Notice how this moves between demonstration and composing together. Notice how it builds in opportunities for oral rehearsal – pupils building structures in their own minds and testing them on a partner.

- The next stage will be to write, and give a running commentary on the decisions you are making, how you reject certain words and ideas (too vague, too formal, not technical enough), modelling all the time the kind of decisions that writers make.

Gradually we will move towards independent writing whereby pupils start to write their own version of a text. Those without confidence might be given a template or writing frame. All will benefit from a reminder of key conventions and vocabulary.

In this way we demonstrate that the teaching of writing – like the other main strands of this book – are about taking what we do implicitly and making them explicit. It's not literacy: it's just what good teachers do.

TALKING POINTS
- Do you use this approach?
- Which parts are most or least relevant for your work?

Helping pupils to write better

The default written style for lots of our pupils will be sentences that are too long and expressed in a conversational or colloquial tone. Thus you'll read sentences like this: 'We started the experiment by designing what we had to do and making a plan which we then checked and then we had to decide on what equipment to use . . .' This is the kind of writing pupils produce. While it's accurate, it lacks authority and control and precision.

That's why the best advice we can give students – before they write – includes:

● Use paragraphs.

● Use some short sentences and some long sentences.

● Vary the openings of your sentences (so that they don't all begin with 'The problem was' or 'I think that').

● Use connectives other than 'and', 'but' and 'so' to join up ideas.

● Write as if you are a reader: make your writing as clear and informative as possible for your reader.

It may be useful to have some specific advice on display in your classroom to support the process of making pupils' writing more engaging, such as:

Varying the openings of sentences:

- Start with a verb ending in 'ing' ('Thinking about the problem, we can see . . .').

- Start with a verb ending in 'ed' ('Frustrated about the situation, Napoleon decides . . .').

- Start with an adverbial (a word or phrase describing time or place or manner, e.g. 'Earlier in the process, Behind the scenes . . .').

Using a wider range of connectives:

- Adding: and, also, as well as, moreover, too.

- Cause and effect: because, so, therefore, thus, consequently.

- Sequencing: next, then, first, finally, meanwhile, before, after.

- Qualifying: however, although, unless, except, if, as long as, apart from, yet.

- Emphasising: above all, in particular, especially, significantly, indeed, notably.

- Illustrating: for example, such as, for instance, as revealed by, in the case of.

- Comparing: equally, in the same way, similarly, likewise, as with, like.

- Contrasting: whereas, instead of, alternatively, otherwise, unlike, on the other hand.

How to write a recount

Essentials:

- Recounts re-tell past events.
- They usually aim to inform or entertain the reader.
- We use them in English, Geography, History, the Social Sciences, ICT and PE.
- Tasks may include: 'write a report', 'write a diary', 'write an account of'.

Key features:

- Recounts normally start by setting the scene, saying something about: what? where? when? how?
- This is followed by a series of events, in the order that they happened (CHRONOLOGICAL ORDER).
- The first sentence may be a 'topic sentence' clearly showing what the text will be about ('This is a report about my visit to the art gallery').
- The final paragraph may be more detached, giving an overview of the subject or evaluating it ('Overall, I learnt a great deal from this visit . . .').

- Recounts are written in the PAST TENSE with the ACTIVE VOICE ('We approached the house by . . .' rather than 'The house was approached by . . .').

- They use CONNECTIVES related to *time* (e.g. 'after', 'then', 'next', 'meanwhile') to *cause* (e.g. 'because', 'since') or to *contrast* (e.g. 'however', 'although', 'nonetheless').

- They focus on specific people or events, not general topics.

- They use the *first person* ('I', 'we') in autobiography and fiction; otherwise they use the *third person* ('he', 'she', 'it', 'they').

- They use vocabulary appropriate to the subject.

Teaching implications

Pupils find recounts pretty straightforward. Part of the teacher's skill is to get them to (a) develop a more impersonal style (not including 'I' or 'me' in every sentence); getting them to vary sentence lengths and sentence starters (think -ed, -ing, -ly); and getting them not to use the first word that comes to mind (alternatives to 'this was a *good* visit': interesting, lively, fascinating, momentous, thought-provoking, fabulous, inspiring, and so on).

How to write analytically

Essentials:

- An analysis is an intellectual account of a process or a response to something seen or read.
- They are usually written to inform or persuade the reader.
- We use them in English, Design Technology, Music, History, Science, Drama, Media Studies.
- They usually call for a more detached and less personal approach than a recount.

Key features:

- The starting point will often be a statement of what is intended – a sentence or paragraph that sets out what the writer hopes to achieve.
- The best analyses will avoid a chronological sequence – the writer will avoid simply retelling the story that is being analysed. It may be organised instead by theme.
- It will provide evidence to support points made.
- Generally in the *third person* ('he', 'she', 'it', 'they'); may use *first person* ('I') to give own views.
- Can use either *past* or *present* tense.

● The *active voice* is probably more usual (e.g. 'We added the potassium') although the *passive* (e.g. 'Potassium was added') may be used.

● *Connectives* of *comparison* (e.g. 'whereas', 'though', 'while', 'unless', 'on the other hand') used to exemplify (e.g. 'this shows that').

● Uses critical vocabulary appropriate to subject.

Teaching implications

This is where we can especially help our word-poor pupils. The language and conventions of analytical writing are often the most alien compared to the language some of our pupils will use at home. Good analytical writing tends to prioritise an impersonal voice (ways of avoiding 'I' and 'me') and more complex, Latinate vocabulary ('significant' rather than 'big').

Pupils need to see more than models and samples: they need to watch us writing and commenting on how we are doing it, the decisions we are making. In this way we will begin to demystify a form of writing which, to some pupils, will feel alien and unattainable.

How to write discursively

Essentials:

- Discursive writing aims to present arguments and information, weighing up different points of view before reaching a conclusion.

- It is different from polemical writing, which is much more opinionated and shows less sense of trying to balance ideas.

- Discursive writing is found in History, English, Science, Social Sciences and RE.

Key features:

- Start with a statement of the issue under discussion.

- Summarise or outline the main arguments as you see them.

- Provide arguments to support one side of the case. Give examples and evidence.

- Provide arguments to support the opposing view. Give examples and evidence.

- Come to a conclusion about which side you recommend.

- Use the *present tense* and usually the *third person.*

- Mostly written in the *active voice.*

- May use *rhetorical questions*, e.g. 'Is this fair?'

● Connectives *contrast* and *compare* and relate to *logic,* e.g. 'as a result', 'alternatively', 'however', 'for example'.

● Tend to use general terms rather than specific ones, e.g., 'many people suggest that. . .'.

Teaching implications

Pupils will often benefit from a writing frame that helps them visualise how to structure their writing. The sense of balance in discursive writing comes from looking systematically at different viewpoints: a structure that moves from one idea to another helps to build this sense of logical argument.

Pupils should be nudged away from overly emotive language ('Use of animals in sport is a bad thing') to a more nuanced approach. This may involve use of modal verbs ('might', 'may', 'could', 'should', 'would'), which can add a tone of tentativeness ('Use of animals in sport may seem wrong . . .').

Pupils should also be encouraged to reject the first word they think of ('bad') and be prompted to think of alternatives ('cruel', 'horrible', 'vindictive', 'inappropriate', 'harmful', 'violent', 'vicious') and then encouraged to see which best fits the context.

How to write to evaluate

Essentials:

- Evaluations describe a process or experiment and then arrive at a judgement.
- Often they are analytical, detailed and impersonal.
- We use them in Drama, Science, Design Technology, Social Sciences and ICT.

Key features:

- May be in list form and include strengths and weaknesses, followed by a summary and targets for the future.
- May use organisational devices such as subheadings to give a more technical, scientific feel.
- May use bullet points and boxed information to summarise key points.
- Written in the *first person* ('I') using *past, present* and *future tenses* appropriately.
- Probably written in the *active voice*, but will aim to use an impersonal style – an avoidance of 'I' and 'we'.
- *Connectives* used to *balance* strengths and weaknesses (e.g. 'although', 'however', 'still', 'on the other hand') and to indicate

use of *evidence* (e.g. 'as in . . .', 'I know this because . . .', 'This shows that . . .').

● Uses technical vocabulary.

Teaching implications

Pupils often misunderstand an instruction to write an evaluation. They think that they are being asked to write a personal response, to give their opinion about something. In reality, most evaluations will chiefly comprise an objective, detached account of how something was made or developed. The secret here is to make it impersonal by avoiding overuse of 'I' and 'me'.

The personal response part comes towards the end: 'I learnt a lot from this process . . .'. It may also be worth encouraging pupils to explore the effect of the pronoun 'we' over 'I'. In some writing – say an English or History essay – this can create a sense of greater authority: 'we can see from this process that . . .'.

As always, pupils need to see us modelling the process of writing.

Writing to explain

Essentials:

- Explanations are designed to show our knowledge and help others to understand: they usually describe ideas or processes.
- We use them in most subjects, perhaps especially the Social Sciences, Science, Design Technology, Home Economics, PE and RE.
- The most common form of explanation text is the essay.

Key features:

- Explanations will often start with a general statement to introduce the topic being explained.
- They follow a set of logical steps – in the correct order – or else the process may not work.
- Usually written in the *present tense* and in *chronological order*.
- They use connectives that are *sequential* (e.g. 'then', 'next'), *causal* (e.g. 'because', 'so') and *comparative* (e.g. 'although', 'in contrast').
- They may use *imperative verbs* (commands) if they are teaching or instructing the reader (e.g. 'First, take the two sides of the paper and fold them together').

- Written in the *third person* ('he', 'she', 'it', 'they') and the *active voice.*

- Vocabulary may be straightforward, to give clarity, but sometimes more complex to demonstrate understanding.

Teaching implications

Explanations benefit hugely from a mix of short and longer sentences. Starting and ending paragraphs with short sentences, or rhetorical questions ('How does the engine work?') can bring real clarity.

Short paragraphs and use of typographical features, such as bullet points can, again, help the reader.

Writing to inform

Essentials:

- This ought to be writing at its clearest – a text-type designed to give information about a topic.
- It is also designed to illustrate the writer's understanding of the concept.
- Most subjects will expect pupils to do some writing to inform, but especially those where there is a need to convey more complex concepts.

Key features:

- It is clear, factual and impersonal.
- May include diagrams, illustrations and tables to break up information, draw in the reader and replace text.
- It is *non-chronological* and written in the *present tense*.
- Opens with a general statement; other information is divided into categories.
- May include an index, glossary, notes, references, table of contents.
- *Third person* ('he', 'she', 'it', 'they'); the *active* alternates with the *passive voice* ('The thermostat *controls* the temperature./ The temperature *is controlled* by the thermostat.').

- Sentences tend to be short and clear.

- *Connectives* emphasise *sequence, cause and effect* and *comparison.*

- *Questions* are used to interest the reader.

- Makes use of subheadings.

- Vocabulary is precise and technical terms relate to the subject matter.

- It is *impersonal* – about the subject rather than the writer.

Teaching implications

This is the form of writing in which to hammer out our perennial basics – short and longer sentences; a variety of formal and informal words; short paragraphs.

Pupils can practise by being given a dense or complicated text and being asked to simplify it, presenting it in their own words in a restricted amount of space.

Show them how you would approach the task, and demonstrate the way in which certain layout features – such as boxes, sub-headings and bullet points – can reinforce a sense of clarity for the reader.

Writing instructions

Essentials:

- Instructions require us to write directly to our reader. In this way our writing is focused not on ourselves and our opinion, but on the needs of our reader.
- Most importantly this will entail the use of imperative verbs – commands.
- A logical, step-by-step approach to organising ideas will be essential too.

Key features:

- Instructions are clear and brief with specific language.
- They start with an aim or goal – what is to be achieved in the writing.
- This is followed by a list of what is needed.
- Next comes the method – the steps to achieve this goal.
- Written in *chronological order* and the *present tense* using *imperative verbs*.
- May use bullet points.
- The reader is generally referred to as 'you'.

- Some instructions require an evaluation of the success of the process.
- Sometimes a diagram or photograph will be helpful.

Teaching implications

It's worth looking at lots of different models of instructional writing before asking pupils to get started. Get them comparing leaflets on using a new phone or recipes, evaluating them for clarity and identifying key features.

There are lots of easy activities that can be done in class to build pupils' understanding of the text type. Get them to give each other instructions on how to tie a tie, or make tea, or construct a paper aeroplane. Then get them thinking about how they could use layout features, sentences and words to provide written instructions that are as clear as possible.

Once you get into the topic in detail, make sure they see you writing and, as you do so, articulate some of the decisions you are making.

Writing to persuade

Essentials:

- This isn't discursive writing: it's not necessarily about presenting a balanced case.
- It's about convincing your reader that you are right.
- That may be in an article, a leaflet or a speech.

Key features:

- Persuasive writing normally starts by stating the proposition to be argued (e.g. 'Animals should never be killed to provide food for humans').
- The arguments to back this up should follow in logical order.
- Each point should be backed up by evidence.
- The argument should be summarised at the end.
- Arguments usually use the *present tense*.
- They focus on the general issues and then elaborate through specific examples.
- They use *connectives*, which logically present the argument (e.g. 'so', 'therefore', 'because').
- Vocabulary can be technical, depending on the audience.
- It includes rhetorical questions

● Emotive language should be used.

● Repetition can be used for impact.

● Suggests the majority agree with the writer (e.g. 'Everyone knows . . .').

Teaching implications

Persuasive writing can prove trickier to teach than we expect. Our pupils may think that it's all merely about opinion – about saying what they think. In fact, of course, good persuasive writing is clever, subtle and often funny. Read Jeremy Clarkson's articles to observe the way the reader's attention is first grabbed. Look at leaflets selling products or persuading us to support a campaign.

In other words, immerse pupils in examples of the text type, reading, cataloguing and comparing before they start to write – a process which (as ever) must involve you being seen to do some demonstration writing.

Writing to report

Essentials:

- Be clear on the difference between a report and a recount:
    - A recount is a chronological report that will describe a sequence of events in order.
    - A report is often more dispassionate, more detached, summarising a finding or discovery.

Key features:

- The style of a report is determined by its purpose. Some may be closer in style to a recount.
- They usually start with a general opening (e.g. 'The frog is an amphibian . . .').
- They move on to being more specific and technical and are likely to contain technical vocabulary.
- They describe qualities and functions, habits and behaviours (e.g. 'Cats have retractile claws. This enables them to catch their prey and keep hold of it.').
- They are usually written in the *present tense*.
- They are *non-chronological*.
- They focus on groups or general aspects.

- They use *descriptive* language that is *factual* and *accurate* – not emotive.

- They use *action verbs* (e.g. 'rises', 'changes').

- They use a formal style involving the *first person* ('I', 'we').

Teaching implications

This is where pupils benefit from seeing how you develop an impersonal style. They may think that this means writing in a style that is complicated. In fact, a good report will be clear and accessible. But, more often than not, it will avoid using 'I' and 'me' too frequently and will, instead, perhaps opt for the more authoritative 'we'.

Pupils will benefit also from seeing you make explicit the way you choose whether a particular word is relevant – whether it is formal enough, too formal, technical or obscure.

In demonstrating how to write a report we should aim to articulate those things we do implicitly.

Glossary of grammatical terms

I've debated whether to include this. Since our theme is 'Don't call it literacy!' I don't want to undermine that message by suggesting that we need every teacher to know what an adverbial (or whatever) is. On the other hand, I'm suggesting that it's every teacher's responsibility to make explicit the skills we use implicitly when speaking, listening, reading and writing in our subject, and in study more generally.

To be able to describe those processes more accurately, the glossary may prove helpful and interesting. In my own teaching I now tend to use more technical language with students, rather as I imagine a teacher of Science does in her subject. In fact, I wrote this glossary originally to use with my students. But – most emphatically – it is definitely not being presented as an end in itself.

Appendices

-ed verbs	Grammar: A participle that can be used at the start of two-part sentences: 'Frustrated, he sat down'.
-ing verbs	Grammar: A participle, which can be used at the start of two-part sentences: 'Falling, the boy shouted for help'.
Active verb	Grammar: In English verbs can be in either the active or the passive voice. In a sentence in the active, the person or thing that performed the action is the subject of the verb – e.g. 'He announced the news' – whereas the passive would be 'the news was announced by him'.
Adjective	Grammar: An adjective modifies a noun. It describes the quality, state or action that a noun refers to – such as 'the *strange* story', 'the *red* sky' and 'the *mysterious* stranger'.
Adverbials	Grammar: A group of words, which serve like an adverb, describing how or when something happened – e.g. '*Before the play*, I saw the car' and '*At the same moment*, the clock chimed'.
Agent	Grammar: The agent is the person or thing that performs the action described by a verb. In both of these sentences the agent is 'the snow': 'The snow fell heavily that night' and 'Her path was covered by the snow'.
Alliteration	Writing technique: Repetition of the first sound in two or more words or phrases – 'the wild winds of winter'. It is used in poetry, advertising and newspaper headlines.
Clause	Grammar: A group of words containing a verb that are the building blocks of sentences. This sentence contains two independent clauses (they can stand on their own): 'I like cats, but I really love dogs'. This sentence contains one independent and one dependent clause (it cannot stand on its own): 'She shouted, waving her fist violently'.
Cohesion	Grammar: The way ideas are linked within a text – e.g. use of pronouns to refer back to something or someone ('Dad arrived. I saw *him* get out of the car' and use of discourse markers: 'An earlier idea was . . .'.
Colon	Punctuation: Used to signal that the word introduces a further comment, explanation or quotation.
Comparatives	Grammar: An adjective that compares the qualities of two or more nouns – e.g. 'this car is faster/slower; more efficient/less efficient'.
Contraction	Grammar: In English we can shorten some words by dropping out certain letters – e.g. 'is not' becomes 'isn't'.

They can be helpful in more informal writing and speech.

Convention

Writing technique: A technique or approach used for a certain type of writing – e.g. there is a convention that newspaper headlines use the present rather than past tense ('Ship Sinks' rather than 'Ship Sank').

Coordination

Grammar: Linking grammatical units that have the same status or wealth – e.g. 'I like fish and I like chips' has two clauses, which could be written the other way round – neither is more important than the other.

Dialect

Language knowledge: A variety of language used in a particular region or by a particular group – e.g. American English.

Exclamation

Writing technique: A sudden cry or outburst expressing surprise or shock. It contrasts with statements, questions and commands.

Exclamation mark

Punctuation mark: Used to demonstrate surprise or shock. In general, aim to use it in dialogue rather than in writing generally.

Front-shifting (or fronting)

Grammar: Moving an element of a sentence to the front to add emphasis – e.g. 'Some things you forget. Other things you remember' (as opposed to 'You forget some things. You remember other things').

Imperative verbs

Grammar: A command – e.g. 'Watch out', 'Buy one today'.

Impersonal style

Writing technique: Writing that avoids stating the 'agent' – e.g. 'The author's techniques are complex' is more impersonal than 'I think the author's techniques are complex'.

Informal

Writing technique: We make writing more informal by choosing more colloquial language (e.g. 'the book is brilliant' rather than 'the book is impressive') and by using contracted forms (e.g. 'I'm' instead of 'I am').

Intonation

Language knowledge: The way we change our pitch when we speak (moving our voice up and down).

Modal verb

Grammar: A verb that signals our mood or attitude – e.g. 'might', 'could', 'will', 'may', 'should'.

Modification

Grammar: The way we add detail to our writing – e.g. in 'the fierce teacher' the noun 'teacher' is premodified by the adjective 'fierce'; in 'the car swerved suddenly' the verb 'swerved' is postmodified by the adverb 'suddenly'.

Passive voice

Grammar: A way of writing that avoids the agent of an action – e.g. 'the man was attacked by the dog' (passive voice) rather than 'the dog attacked the man' (active).

Appendices

Past tense	Grammar: The way we choose verbs to show our topic takes place or is set in the past – e.g. 'the hyena howled', 'the hyena was howling', 'the hyena had howled'.
Polysyllabic	Grammar: A word containing more than one syllable – e.g. 'helicopter' contains four syllables: 'hel-i-cop-ter'.
Present tense	Grammar: The way we choose verbs to show that our topic takes place in the present – e.g. 'he laughs', 'he is laughing'.
Punctuation	Language knowledge: Signs used in written language to separate elements (e.g. capital letters and full stops show the start and end of sentences), and to signal an attitude or relationship (an apostrophe can show that something belongs to someone).
Puns	Language knowledge: A play on words, sometimes on different senses of the same word and sometimes on the similar sense or sound of different words – e.g. 'The oil well driller had a *boring* job'.
Question	Grammar: A sentence that asks for information or for a response. A rhetorical question is often used to involve the reader by asking a question to which no specific answer is required. It is a question for effect – e.g. 'Can this ever be truly fair?'
Sentence	Grammar: A unit of meaning that makes sense on its own: it begins with a capital letter and ends with a full stop, question mark or exclamation mark.
Specialist	Language knowledge: One way of responding to the vocabulary in a text is to see whether it is specialist (e.g. 'cardiograph') or non-specialist ('heart monitor'). The writer's choice of vocabulary will help you to see who the audience might be (general readers or people with knowledge of the subject).
Statement	Grammar: A sentence that reports information. In grammar we often call these 'declarative sentences' compared to, say, imperatives (instructions) and interrogatives (questions) – e.g. 'The night was warm and welcoming'.
Subordination	Grammar: One grammatical element being dependant on another (meaning that it cannot stand on its own) – e.g. in 'The computer *that was making a strange sound* suddenly exploded' the clause 'that was making a strange sound' is subordinate, part of the main clause ('The computer suddenly exploded').
Superlatives	Grammar: An adjective or adverb used to show the superior quality of something – e.g. 'best/most/happiest'.

Glossary of grammatical terms

Suspense	Writing technique: The way writers hold back information to keep readers guessing what will happen next.
Synonym	Grammar: A word with a similar meaning to another word – e.g. 'big', 'large', 'bulky', 'major', 'important', 'significant'.
Telegraphic style	Grammar: A style of writing that deletes some words to make the meaning more concentrated. Newspaper and magazine headlines often use this approach.
Tension	Writing technique: See suspense.
Topic sentence	Writing technique: A sentence often used at the beginning of a piece of writing to summarise the whole story – e.g. 'an 85-year-old woman narrowly escaped from a flaming room seconds before it collapsed today'. Notice how the sentence tells us something about 'who', 'where', 'what' and 'when'.
Viewpoint	Writing technique: Also known as 'point of view', this describes the way a writer recounts a story – e.g. first person ('I'), second person ('you') and third person ('she/he/they').
Vocabulary	Language knowledge: The range of words known by a person. In general, knowing more words helps us to express ideas more precisely.

Subject-by-subject spelling lists

Science
absorb
acid
alkaline
amphibian
apparatus
chemical
circulate/circulation
combustion
condensation
cycle
digest/digestion
disperse/dispersal
dissolve
distil/distillation
element
evaporation
exchange
freeze
frequency
friction
function
growth
hazard
insect
laboratory
liquid
mammal
method
nutrient
organism
oxygen

particles
predator
reproduce
respire/respiration
solution
temperature
thermometer
vertebrate
vessel

Maths
addition
angle
amount
approximately
average
axis
calculate
centimetre
circumference
co-ordinate
decimal
degree
diameter
digit
divide/division
enough
equilateral
estimate
fraction
graph
guess

horizontal
isosceles
kilogram
litre
measure
metre
minus
multiply/multiplication
negative
parallel/parallelogram
perimeter
perpendicular
positive
quadrilateral
radius
regular
rhombus
rotate/rotation
square
subtraction
symmetry/symmetrical
triangle/triangular
vertical
volume
weight

History
agriculture/agricultural
bias
castle
cathedral
Catholic
chronology/chronological
citizen
civilisation
colony/colonisation
conflict
constitution/constitutional
contradict/contradiction
current
defence
disease
document
dynasty
economy/economic/al
emigration
government
immigrant
imperial/imperialism

independence
invasion
motive
parliament
politics/political
priest
propaganda
Protestant
rebel/rebellion
reign
religious
republic
revolt/revolution
siege
source
trade
traitor

Geography
abroad
amenity
atlas
authority
climate
contour
country
county
desert
employment
erosion
estuary
function
globe
habitat
infrastructure
international
landscape
latitude
location
longitude
nation/national
physical
pollution
poverty
provision
region/regional
rural
settlement
situation

Appendices

tourist/tourism
transport/transportation
urban
wealth
weather

RE
baptism
Bible/biblical
Buddhist/Buddhism
burial
celebrate/celebration
ceremony
Christian
commandment
commitment
creation
disciple
faith
festival
funeral
Hindu/Hinduism
hymn
immoral/immorality
Islam
Israel
Judaism/Jewish
marriage
miracle
moral/morality
Muslim
parable
pilgrim/pilgrimage
pray/prayer
prejudice
prophet
religious/religion
shrine
sign
Sikh/Sikhism
special
spirit/spiritual
symbol
synagogue
temple
wedding
worship

Music
choir
chord
chromatic
composition/conductor
crotchet
dynamics
harmony
instrument/instrumental
interval
lyric
major
melody
minim
minor
musician
octave
orchestra/orchestral
ostinato
percussion
pitch
quaver
rhythm
scale
score
semibreve
synchronise
syncopation
tempo
ternary
timbre
triad
vocal

Drama
applause
character/characteristic
costume
curtain
director
dramatise
entrance
exit
freeze
improvise
inspire
lighting
movement

perform/performance
playwright
position
rehearse/rehearsal
role
scene/scenario
script
share
spotlight
stage
theatre/theatrical

PSHE
able/ability
achieve/achievement
addict/addiction
approve/approval
communication
control
dependant/dependency
discipline
discussion
effort
emotion/emotional
encourage/encouragement
gender
generous/generosity
involve/involvement
prefer/preference
pressure
racism/racist
reality
relationship
represent/representative
reward
sanction
sexism/sexist
stereotype

PE
active/activity
agile/agility
athletic/athlete
bicep
exercise
field
gym/gymnastic
hamstring
injury

league
medicine
mobile/mobility
muscle
personal
pitch
quadriceps
qualify
relay
squad
tactic
tournament
triceps

Art
abstract
acrylic
charcoal
collage
collection
colour
crosshatch
dimension
display
easel
exhibition
foreground
frieze
gallery
highlight
illusion
impasto
kiln
landscape
palette
pastel
perspective
portrait
sketch
spectrum

D and T
aesthetic
brief
carbohydrate
component
design
diet
disassemble

Appendices

evaluation
fabric
fibre
flour
flowchart
hygiene
ingredient
innovation
knife/knives
linen
machine
manufacture
mineral
natural
nutrition
polyester
portfolio
presentation
production
protein
recipe
sew
specification
technology
tension
textile
vitamin

ICT
binary
byte
cable
cartridge
CD-Rom
computer
connect/connection
cursor
data/database
delete
disk
document
electronic
graphic
hardware
icon
input
interactive
interface
Internet

justify
keyboard
megabyte
memory
modem
module
monitor
multimedia
network
output
password
preview
processor
program
scanner
sensor
server
software
spreadsheet
virus

Library
Alphabet/alphabetical
anthology
article
author
catalogue
classification
content
copyright
dictionary
editor
encyclopaedia
extract
fantasy
genre
glossary
index
irrelevant/irrelevance
librarian
magazine
non-fiction
novel
photocopy
publisher
relevant/relevance
romance
section
series

system
thesaurus

English
advertise/advertisement
alliteration
apostrophe
atmosphere
chorus
clause
cliché
comma
comparison
conjunction
consonant
dialogue
exclamation
expression
figurative
genre
grammar
imagery

metaphor
myth
narrative/narrator
onomatopoeia
pamphlet
paragraph
personification
playwright
plural
prefix
preposition
resolution
rhyme
scene
simile
soliloquy
subordinate
suffix
synonym
tabloid
vocabulary
vowel

Week-by-week spellings

a lot
abstract
acceptable
accidentally
accommodation
acquire
actually
advertisement
advise
advice
affect
effect
allowed
aloud
analysis
apostrophe
argument
article
assessment
atmosphere
audible
audience
autumn
beautiful
beginning
believe
beneath
braking
breaking
brief
business
calendar

category
caught
celebration
centimetre
ceremony
changeable
characterisation
chocolate
chord
chronological
civilisation
colour
column
commandment
commitment
committed
concentration
conclusion
conscience
conscious
conscientious
consequence
continuous
defence
definitely
development
disappear
disappoint
disciple
discipline
disease
document

embarrassment
environment
evaluation
evidence
exceed
exhibition
existence
experience
explanation
February
fierce
foreign
forty
fulfil
gauge
government
grammar
grateful
guarantee
guard
happened
height
humorous
hygiene
imagery
imaginary
immediate
immorality
improvise
independent
indispensable
ingredient
innovation
intelligence
interesting
interrupt
involvement
isosceles
issue
its/it's
knowledge
liaison
library
lonely
manoeuvre
material
meanwhile
medieval
metaphor

metre
millennium
miniature
mischievous
modern
moreover
necessary
noticeable
occasionally
occurrence
onomatopoeia
original
outrageous
parallel
parliament
participation
particles
pattern
peaceful
peer
people
percussion
performance
permanent
perpendicular
perseverance
personal
personnel
personification
persuade
physical
playwright
possession
potential
practise
practice
precede
preparation
principal
principle
prioritise
privilege
process
proportion
proposition
protein
publicly
questionnaire
queue

Appendices

quiet
quite
reaction
receipt
receive
recipe
recommend
reference
referred
relevant
relief
rhyme
rhythm
safety
scene
separate
sequence
sights
simile
sincerely
sites
skilful

source
straight
strategy
strength
surely
surprise
their
there
they're
threw
through
tomorrow
twelfth
unfortunately
until
vacuum
weather
weird
whether
wonderful
yacht

Reading list

A small number of books have had a big influence on me.

On teaching

These are the books that give the most helpful advice on being a teacher:

- Beadle, P. (2010) *How to teach*, Carmarthen: Crown House Publishing.
  Funny, feisty and packed with hugely useful hints and ideas.

- Gilbert, I. (forthcoming) *Essential motivation in the classroom*, London: Routledge.
  Wise and inspiring: I think this is one of the best books that has been published for teachers in the past 10 years.

- Smith, J. (2010) *The lazy teacher's handbook*, Carmarthen: Crown House Publishing.
  The title is slightly off-putting, but it's a great book for reassuring us that simple steps can help pupils to learn better.

- Lemov, D. (2010) *Teach like a champion*, San Francisco, CA: John Wiley & Sons.
  An American guide to the tiny skills that teachers can use to build the confidence and then progress of their pupils. It comes with a demonstration DVD.

- Claxton, G. (2008) *What's the point of school? Rediscovering the heart of education*, London: Oneworld.

  Wise reminder in an age of targets and tests of what real learning is about.

- Marland, M. (1975) *The craft of the classroom*, London: Heinemann.

  With his passion for teaching, his expertise in literacy and his extraordinary generosity, Marland remains a hero of mine, and this is the book that convinced me that I should become a teacher.

Language and literacy

I've read lots of language books. These are the ones that are most provocative or thought-provoking:

- Deutscher, G. (2010) *Through the language glass*, Portsmouth, NH: Heinemann.

  Fascinating account of the link between the language we use and whether this shapes the way we perceive the world.

- Hitchings, H. (2011) *The language wars: A history of proper English*, London: John Murray.

  A compelling account of the battles between prescriptivists and descriptivists to constrain or liberate English.

- Osborne, J. and Lehr, F. (eds) (1998) *Literacy for all*, New York: Guilford Press.

  Not an entertaining read, but lots of informative insights into current literacy issues.

- Heffer, S. (2010) *Strictly English*, London: Random House.

  Heffer's strong views on language (we should order a 'panino' [singular], not 'a panini' [plural], he insists) is by turns funny, irritating and always provocative.

- Miller, G. (2001) *The mating mind: How sexual choice shaped the evolution of human nature*, London: Heinemann.

  A quirkily entertaining book, which contains insights into how we are judged by our vocabulary.

- Lamb, S. E. (1998) *How to write it*, New York: Ten Speed Press.

  An astonishing compendium from America of guidance on how to write pretty much anything.

- Mercer, N. and Hodgkinson, S. (2008) *Exploring talk in school*, London: Sage.

  The most useful guide to using talk in the classroom. Superb.

- Geary, J. (2011) *I is an other*, London: HarperCollins.

  Fascinating insight into the richly metaphorical nature of our language.

Education and related topics

- Brooks, D. (2011) *The social animal: A story of how success happens*, London: Random House.

  Fashionable and eminently readable book about how our life chances can be shaped by the right school and social environment.

- Hirsch, E. D. (1996) *The schools we need and why we don't have them*, New York: Anchor Books.

  On why knowledge is like Velcro and why we should teach our pupils as much knowledge as possible: the more they know the easier they will find it to learn.

- Gladwell, M. (2006) *Blink: The power of thinking without thinking*. London: Allen Lane.

  Quirky, entertaining stuff on how first impressions (including by teachers) matter.

Appendices

- Rigney, D. (2010) *The Matthew Effect: How advantage begets further advantage*, New York: Columbia University Press.

  In many ways, my core text. It's not an entertaining read, but its message (summarised in the subtitle) is profound.

- Marzano, R. J. (2004) *Building background knowledge for academic achievement*, Alexandria, VA: ASCD.

  Does what he says: like Hirsch, he argues for more teaching of knowledge.

- Young, M. F. D. (2008) *Bringing knowledge back in*, London: Routledge.

  Same theme: the link between knowledge and vocabulary and power.

Afterword

I've written this book quickly over a few weeks and in doing so I realise that actually it's been brewing inside me for many years.

In that time I have had the privilege of working with, talking to and learning from hundreds of teachers. I still find it an extraordinary privilege to watch a great teacher at work, and I want to thank all of them – all of you – for the ideas, refinements to ideas, and debates that you have shared. I have met you in the schools I have worked in, those I have spoken to on training days, through conferences and on Twitter. I have loved the generosity of people sharing ideas, sending resources, and collaborating on new approaches. All of my ideas are really yours.

I hope that this book proves useful to you in pulling some of those approaches together in one place, that the tone isn't too irksome, so that together we can push on with our mission of helping both the word-rich and the word-poor to feel the power and beauty and endless creativity of language – to join us, in other words, as paid-up members of the Literacy Club. Or whatever we choose to call it.

Geoff Barton

Index

Index

Index

Index